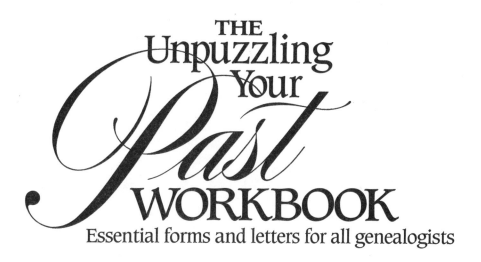

THE Unpuzzling Your Past WORKBOOK

Essential forms and letters for all genealogists

EMILY ANNE CROOM

BETTERWAY BOOKS
CINCINNATI, OHIO

The Unpuzzling Your Past Workbook. Copyright © 1996 by Emily Anne Croom. Printed and bound in the United States of America. All rights reserved. No part of this book may be reproduced in any form or by any electronic or mechanical means including information storage and retrieval systems without permission in writing from the publisher, except by a reviewer, who may quote brief passages in a review, or by the purchaser, who may copy the blank forms for his or her personal use. Published by Betterway Books, an imprint of F&W Publications, Inc., 1507 Dana Avenue, Cincinnati, Ohio 45207. (800) 289-0963. First edition.

Other fine Betterway Books are available from your local bookstore or direct from the publisher.

00 99 98 97   5 4 3 2

ISBN 1-55870-423-X

Edited by Argie J. Manolis
Cover photography by Pamela Monfort Braun, Bronze Photography

The map appearing on pages 37, 309 and 311 has been supplied by the Gaylord Stickle Company, 2715 Bissonnet, Suite 205, Houston, TX 77005.

Betterway Books are available for sales promotions, premiums and fund-raising use. Special editions or book excerpts can also be created to specification. For details, contact Special Sales Manager, F&W Publications, 1507 Dana Avenue, Cincinnati, Ohio 45207.

TABLE OF CONTENTS

Alphabetical Ancestors by Alphabetical Headings (1)
to index a collection of family group sheets or pedigree charts.

Alphabetical Ancestors by Surname (1)
to index all relatives by the same surname.

Alphabetical Ancestors by Locality (1)
to form a master list of all ancestors from one location (county, state, etc.).

Index to Workshop Notes and Handouts, *with* alphabetical headings given (1)
to index notes and handouts collected from seminars and workshops.

Index to Workshop Notes and Handouts, *without* alphabetical headings provided (1)
to allow searchers to develop their own index or for already large collections.

Notes (3)
to encourage proper documentation of notes and facilitate notetaking.

Deed Abstract (3)
to facilitate abstracting deed records and encourage thoroughness.

Census Forms
to expedite census extraction and encourage thoroughness.
1790 Census (4)
1800–1810 Census (4)
1820 Census (4)
1830–1840 Census—Part 1 (4)
1830 Census—Part 2 (4)
1840 Census—Part 2 (4)
1850 Census (5)
1860 Census (5)
1850–1860 Slave Schedules (5)

1870 Census (5)
1880 Census (5)
1900 Census (5)
1910 Census (5)
1920 Census (5)

Interview Forms
to aid in interviewing relatives for family history in the twentieth century.
Pre-1930 Period (1)
Depression–1930s (1)
World War II and the 1940s (1)
Decade of the 1950s (1)
Decade of the 1960s (1)

Family Group Sheet (10)
to present vital statistics and documentation for each nuclear family.

Ahnentafel Table (2)
to compile known ancestors for any one individual.

Five-Generation Chart (2)
to show one individual and four generations of ancestors, with vital statistics.

Ahnentafel Five-Generation Chart (2)
to show any five generations, using ahnentafel identification numbers.

Biographical Outline (4)
to consolidate all information known about one individual, with documentation.

United States Map (2)
to track migrations and residences of ancestral families.

Timelines
to place ancestors into history as an aid to study and comparison.
1600–1800 (1)
1750–1950 (1)

INTRODUCTION

Genealogy is an intriguing, engrossing, captivating, fascinating, popular hobby and profession. In order to be successful, the genealogist must (1) plan and organize and (2) do careful, accurate, thorough research. The genealogist who plans and organizes without good research has no real success, for the results are meaningless. The one who tries to do the appropriate research using little scraps of paper, without planning or organization, finds that success is elusive, literally lost in the shuffle. But the genealogist who plans *and* organizes *and* researches carefully will experience the excitement and gratification of accomplishment. This is true when one finds a great-grandmother's "long-lost" maiden name, proves the identification of the long-sought father or mother of an ancestor, or determines that a certain elusive ancestor was alive in a given year and place. The smallest detail can make the avid genealogist squeal.

If you are relatively new to genealogy, use this book as a workbook to accompany *Unpuzzling Your Past*, as the two are intended to complement each other and the beyond-the-basics *The Genealogist's Companion & Sourcebook*. Both of these books, by Emily Croom, are published by Betterway Books in Cincinnati, Ohio. *Unpuzzling Your Past* and *The Genealogist's Companion & Sourcebook* are primarily concerned with the research aspect of genealogy. This book deals with planning and organization.

A book of genealogical forms has one basic purpose—to help organize research and its results. When we organize our *research*, we tend to be more efficient and more thorough, and our efforts stay focused on our goals. When we organize the *results*, we are in a better position to study and evaluate. We avoid duplicating our efforts, and we have a better picture of where we are in our search. Best of all, we can find our information readily.

Organizing systems are probably more numerous than genealogists, for who has not begun with one system and switched at least once to what seemed a better one? This book does not promote any particular system; each genealogist must develop or adapt one best suited to personal style and needs. The key is to use consistently the system that works best for you.

Many people use three-ring binders for collecting and organizing data, by surname or locality or both. Some transfer notes to file folders, large index cards or computer word processing documents. Many use genealogy computer programs to link known relatives and store basic information on them. Still others use a combination of these systems.

My own preference is three-ring binders, one (or more) for each surname, divided by locality. When the amount of material for one locality outgrows its space, it becomes a separate binder, such as METCALFE-Texas or COLEMAN-Cumberland County, Virginia. What I want in an organizing system is to gather and file notes in one operation, without having to transcribe, sort and file notes once I get home from the library or courthouse. This means that note taking is limited to one surname in one locality per page. I find it helpful to write at the top of each page of notes, usually in the upper right corner, the surname to which the notes pertain: BLAKENEY-Jasper County or SHELBY-South Carolina. In keeping with this practice, many of the forms in the book begin with a title that includes the surname written at the top of the page.

The forms in this book can be used with practically any organizing system. Some, such as the census check, military records checklist, and biographical outline, are indispensable in seeing at a glance what has been done and planning the next step. Others, such as the interview and census forms, are valuable in both the information-gathering and -storage processes. Still others, including family group sheets, five-generation charts and biographical outlines, consolidate information already gathered, evaluated and accepted to give an overall picture of the ancestor(s).

Blank forms make up the bulk of the book. Some appear only once, as master copies from which readers should make photocopies for their own use. Others are provided in multiple copies for your convenience. You may want to keep at least one blank form of each type as a master.

The examples and suggestions which follow are some of the ways these forms can be used. Be creative and adapt them to suit your own needs as you begin or continue unpuzzling your past!

PART ONE

Forms for Planning and Organizing Research— Checklists

Each checklist in this book is a tool to help genealogists focus on a particular aspect of their research. The forms include a census check, a military records checklist, a research planning worksheet (called a problem search form in *Unpuzzling Your Past*), and a contact log. What makes these forms unique is that you can tailor them to your own research. They will guide you to define your problem, to evaluate your progress, and to decide what to do next.

CENSUS CHECK

The census check lets you consolidate census information on any one person. Use one form for information from the decennial federal censuses on that person and another form for colonial, territorial or state census information. Each form allows you to see at a glance

- Where you hope to find the person in each census during his or her lifetime
- Where you *do* find this person
- What problems you have encountered
- Which records you have searched
- Which records remain to be searched
- Ideas for future research

This form does not take the place of the census forms for each federal census, which appear later in this book. Instead, it summarizes your research and records the reference or bibliographic information on each find.

The reference information at the top of the form keeps pertinent vital statistics handy as your search progresses. Example 1 on page 5 is for an ancestor who married four times and outlived all four husbands. Because her name was different in five successive federal censuses, it was helpful to have the marriage information readily available during the census searches. (Fortunately, my grandmother had alerted me to different surnames, so I began my search in the marriage records of the county where this ancestor had lived. By the time I began the census search, I knew Sarah's surname in each census year.)

The column for age provides another perspective to aid in the search and study. Several people by the same name may show up in a given county or state. When searching for your own ancestor, knowing his or her age as well as potential family members can aid in sorting out the candidates. The age to write in the column is the age you believe the person to be on *census day* of the census year. As the instructions to the federal census takers stated, all information they recorded was to be correct as of census day, regardless of when the enumerator actually visited the household. Some enumerators and/or families followed these instructions and some did not. This is one reason we also record the date of the enumerator's visit. For 1790-1820, census day was the first Monday in August. For 1830-1900, it was June 1. Thereafter, census day was April 15 (1910), January 1 (1920) and April 1 (1930-1940). See chapters 12, 13 and 15 in *Unpuzzling Your Past* and chapter 2 of *The Genealogist's Companion & Sourcebook* for further discussion and case studies of census research.

MILITARY RECORDS CHECKLIST

The military records checklist allows you to record each ancestor or person of interest and search the military records appropriate to that person's life. For example, you would not want to spend time searching Civil War service records for an ancestor born in 1855 or 1760. On the other hand, you would not want to overlook a set of potentially helpful records just because "Nobody ever said he was in that war." Lists of corresponding military records to search can be found in such reference books as these:

1. *The Genealogist's Companion & Sourcebook*, by Emily Croom. Cincinnati: Betterway Books, 1994. Chapter 4 surveys microfilm resources available through the National Archives and at many libraries.
2. *Military Service Records: A Select Catalog of National Archives Microfilm Publications.* Washington, DC: National Archives Trust Fund Board, National Archives and Service Administration, 1985. Catalog of descriptions and film numbers, especially helpful in determining which rolls of film you may need to study.
3. *U.S. Military Records: A Guide to Federal & State Sources, Colonial America to the Present*, by James C. Neagles. Salt Lake City: Ancestry Inc., 1994. An excellent resource for genealogists, detailing the kinds of records generated and kept at both state and federal levels, whether microfilmed or not.

Military records concern all the services (army, navy, marines, militia, national guard, coast guard, merchant marine, and eventually, air force), both volunteers and those in regular service. These records deal with many aspects of military business, such as service records, pensions and bounty land warrants, prisoners, deserters, casualties, burials, soldiers' homes, medical and battle reports, courts-martial, the service academies and correspondence. Some federal and state censuses also report certain information about veterans. Thus, many records exist. Each genealogist must decide the extent to which the records may be pertinent to a particular search.

The form furnished here is a general reminder to begin with the service records available from a particular period for ancestors who might have served at that time. If indeed you find an ancestor in one of the services, you may want to investigate further in other kinds of military records, such as those for Civil War prison camps. We must remember that the more recent records are open only to servicemen or women or next of kin. We must also remember that colonial, some Revolutionary, and some Confederate records are found in state rather than federal archives. Ask in the state archives or historical society of your research

area to determine what military records they have, or consult *U.S. Military Records*, listed above.

The checklist can be used in several ways. One option is to limit each form to one surname and search for direct ancestors and their brothers and cousins. Another option is to list all male ancestors from a pedigree chart, regardless of surname, and use the form as a master checklist. (Add females to the checklist as you deem appropriate to your family). To aid in the search, it is helpful to record, with the ancestor's name, his life dates and residences so that you can (1) cross out the wars or service periods for which he was too young, too old or not alive and (2) have a frame of reference for where he may have enlisted, applied for a pension or, for World War I and after, filed his discharge papers at the county courthouse.

In the columns that fall within the subject's life, you could write in his age at the beginning of that conflict or period. Then you can decide whether to spend time searching records for a seventy-five-year-old man or a twelve-year-old child. As the example shows, when the record is found, it can be noted. You can establish your own system, such as using *P* to indicate a pension record, *S* for a service record, *BLW* for bounty land warrant, etc. The example simply uses *pension*, *serv* for service record, and *CSA* for Confederate States of America. Notes in your notebooks and files will detail the search and its results. The checklist is simply a tool to give visual perspective and help make the search more thorough.

As Example 2 shows, a horizontal line through the non-applicable columns is easy to use and does not visually clutter the chart, and a diagonal slash through other columns can indicate a decision not to search due to a person's advanced age, known illness or disability, or absolute certainty that he did not serve. For one man in the example, family *tradition* reports his service in the Revolution, but the searcher has not yet found records to that effect. For another man, a record was found for someone with the same name, but, because the name is common in that family, it has not yet been determined whether it is the same person. However you use the checklist, be creative and let it serve you.

RESEARCH PLANNING WORKSHEET

The research planning worksheet is an aid for planning a search strategy. It is a checklist you create for a specific individual or family, at any point in a search, to help you lay out the beginning steps or deal with the tougher and narrower questions after trying the first sources. Used in conjunction with the contact log explained below, it focuses on a given problem:

- What is the problem to be studied?
- What have you tried (sources, contacts, evaluation) and with what results?
- What questions now need to be asked to find a solution?
- What is your next course of action? (research, sources, contacts, evaluations, crystal ball?)

Of course, the form is not intended to be used as a list of all possible sources for a specific search. Rather, it is a place to list the ones you want to try *next* in your search. Depending on the results, you can continue on a new form to concentrate on a real challenge from new angles or to tackle a different aspect of the same family.

Example 3 reflects an ongoing search for which the first sources—census, tombstone inscriptions, newspapers, marriage records, and successions (probate)—yielded very little information. The most inter-

esting discovery from these sources was the revelation that both mother and daughter had married men named Isaac Croom, uncle and nephew to each other.

CONTACT LOG

A contact log is another planning device and serves as a checklist for personal contacts, such as letters, telephone calls and interviews. It is especially helpful to make such a list early in a search as you gather preliminary information from relatives. However, the form can be used at any point in a search. I like to write down ideas for contacts even if I cannot get to them right away.

Example 4 illustrates a search which had already gathered information from the few remaining relatives and census and was confronted with conflicting vital statistics on a late-nineteenth-century grandfather. Fortunately, I was able to make a number of local inquiries and appointments by telephone. Some of the list I generated in advance. Other contacts I added as the search progressed. For example, two church secretaries suggested other churches to contact which had existed in the time period I was searching.

Census Check on <u>SARAH W. ORGAIN HARRISON TISDALE EVANS SMITH</u>
Name <u>"Grandma Smith"</u>

Birthdate/place <u>3 APRIL 1840 NEAR PARIS, HENRY Co. TN</u>   First Census <u>1840</u>

Father's Name <u>STERLING ORGAIN</u>   Mother's Name <u>MARY E. JONES</u>

Marriage date/place
- m1 <u>JULY 1861, WILLIAMSON Co TX</u>   m1· <u>WILLIAM L. HARRISON</u>
- m2 <u>MAR 1871   "</u>   Spouse m2· <u>J.E. TISDALE (d 1894)</u>
- m3 <u>NOV 1896   "</u>   m3· <u>WILLIAM T. EVANS (d 1905)</u>

Death date/place <u>1 MAY 1928</u>   Burial place <u>STAMFORD, JONES Co TX</u>
- m4 <u>?</u>   m4· <u>JOHN S. SMITH (d 1915)</u>

Census Year	Age	State/Counties Searched ✓=found there x=not found	County Where Found & Notes	Film #, Roll #, E.D., Pg, etc.
1840	2/12	WITH STERLING ORGAIN Madison Co TN x Henry Co TN ✓	All males in family are accounted for in entry. Extra female 5-10 - Who? Daughter?	M 704 roll 522 p 425
1850	9	WITH STERLING ORGAIN Williamson Co TX x Madison Co TN ✓ Henry Co TN x	Age 9 dau listed as Jane. Sister Jane also listed. family 542	M 432 roll 889 pr p 327B wp 654 dist 12
1860	19	WITH STERLING ORGAIN Williamson Co TX ✓	In Round Rock. Kids at home: John, Sterling, Sarah, Benj D.	M 653 roll 1308 p 47 family 304 dwell 295
1870	29	SARAH W. HARRISON widow Williamson Co TX x	not found in county or in Texas index. Haven't found parents either.	M 593
1880	39	SARAH W. TISDALE Williamson Co TX ✓	Precinct 8. printed p 583. JE + Sarah*, his-hers-ours kids + brother Sterling Orgain Jr. *(Sallie)	T 9 roll 1333 e.d. 162 sheet 53 family 459
1900	59	SARAH W. EVANS Williamson Co TX ✓	Precinct 8. Her b-date wrong (May 1837). With them are brother Sterling Jr + son Dick Tisdale! (Sallie)	T 623 roll 1680 e.d. 140 sheet 3A family 53
1910	69	SARAH W. SMITH Bastrop Co TX ✓	In Elgin, m 2 years. Mother of 5, 4 living! With them, brother Sterling + grandson Joseph Metcalfe! (Sarah)	T 624 roll 1529 e.d. 9 sheet 2B dwelling 36
1920	79	SARAH W. SMITH widow Bexar Co w/ Metcalfe x Jones Co w/ Harrison ✓	At 514 E. Reynolds, Stamford w/ son Edward B. Harrison + wife + brother Sterling Jr (84) (Sallie)	T 625 roll 1824 e.d. 128 sheet 6B-7A
/		d 1928	*THESE NOTES ARE ONLY HIGHLIGHTS. THEY DO NOT TAKE THE PLACE OF CENSUS FORMS.*	

UNPUZZLING YOUR PAST WORKBOOK   Example 1

Military Records Checklist for Ancestors of Robert T. Shelby

Ancestor Name & Life Dates	Colonial Wars (state records)	American Revolution 1775–1783 (check state & federal records)	1784–1811	War of 1812 (1812–1815)	Indian Wars 1815–1858	Patriot War 1838	Mexican War 1846–1848	Civil War 1861–1865 (for Confederates, check state & federal records)	Service 1866 forward	Spanish-American War 1898–1899	Philippine Insurrection 1899–1902	World War I 1917–1918	World War II 1941–1945
Evan Shelby NC 1775–1850s MS		No record found	One Evan 3 Reg SC State Troops 37	41+	63	71							
John P. Shelby SC 1818–1900 TX					20		28	CSA Pension + Serv. 43+	48+	80			
George M. Shelby MS 1845–after 1912 TX brother of Travis								CSA Pen. App. Serv. 16+		ill 53	ill 54	d? 72	
Irving R. Shelby GA 1849–1912 TX brother of Travis								not found 16 at end	17+	49	50		
Travis O. Shelby MS 1864–1943 TX										Family knowledge did not serve 34	35	53	77
John Blakeney c1732–1832	check NC, SC			80	84+								
John Blakeney II NC 1758–1848 SC		Pension	No record found 54	No record found 58+	No record found 80	88							
John Blakeney III SC 1791–1876 SC			No record found 21	No record found 25+	No record found 47	55	70						
Stephen J. Ford MS 1839–1885 LA								CSA Serv. POW 22	27				
Samuel David Williamson AL 1827–1911 LA								CSA Service 34	39	71	72		
John Wesley Williamson LA 1879–1956 LA										20		draft regis. 38	62

Callout notes:
- Age at the time
- Horizontal lines indicate period not applicable to this person.
- Slash means we won't look for records in these cases.
- Have found service record + prisoner record – Confederate

Example 2   UNPUZZLING YOUR PAST WORKBOOK

6

Research Planning Worksheet

Maiden name in parentheses

Date ___summer 1992___

Statement of the Problem __to find father of Ann (Robertson) Croom & first husband__
of Elizabeth Robertson Croom. Ann b GA c1836
(m2 LA, 1846)   bro Thos.J. b GA c 1841-42

Questions Related to the Problem:

1. How did Isaac Croom Sr get the land he sold & gave away? Was any of it Elizabeth's? **NO**

2. Can I find any evidence of Elizabeth before or after her 1846 m to Isaac Sr other than 1850 census?

3. What can I find on the Robertson kids or half sister Louisiana (Croom) Harris? Locate any descendants?

4. Do records of neighboring parishes help? Maybe Eliz. came to Caddo Parish <u>after</u> Robertson died.

5. If Robertson died in GA, why would Eliz. come to LA & with whom?

6. Might study witnesses and surety on the 2 marriage records (Eliz. & Ann).

[already searched US census, parish tombstone inscriptions, newspaper, marriages, successions]
↳ *No Isaac or Eliz. in 1860 or 1870. We know Isaac was alive in both years.*
Try next: deeds, tract books, tax records, New Orleans Notarial Archives   *Not found in LA or TX.*

Sources to Try	Results
1. Caddo Parish deeds  *Deed book + page numbers listed as references. Details in notes.*	*Nothing found in deeds (so far) pointing to a Robertson husband/father. Did find* (1) S:855–Thomas J. Robertson in Lafayette Co AR in Dec 1871. (2) S:855,721–Elizabeth's middle initial–C. (3) L:194–Elizabeth alive in Nov 1857. (4) S:721–Elizabeth d by Oct 1871. (5) P:975–Indication that Elizabeth d by April 1868. (6) S:721–Isaac moved to Panola Co Tx by Oct 1871.
2. Panola Co Tx Marriages	*Isaac remarried there, Nov 1868.*
3. Caddo Parish tract books (1995)	*Bureau of Land Mgt. CD-ROM–Automated Land Records. Isaac's land accounted for here & in deeds. Apparently none of it had been Elizabeth's. No Robertson patents in right time period (pre-1846).*
4. New Orleans Notarial Archives	• *must go there – records not microfilmed.* • *need names of notaries from Caddo Parish 1840s–c1870* • *any marriage agreement or family meeting before Elizabeth m Isaac Sr? or anything at all...*

Contact Log # __2__   Surname or Search   GRANDPA KING   d 1941
                                            ALFRED THOMAS KING

Contact plan	Subject	Contact made, date	Results & notes
Call County Clerk	old voter registration records	6 Feb 94	says they don't keep them
Call E. Point GA nat'l archives branch	form for WWI draft	7 Feb 94	sent form
Call Noni	John's new phone #	7 Feb 94	✓
Write Tx DPS	Did Grandpa have driver's license?	8 Feb 94	no records before 1976
Call Trinity Epis. Church - Baytown	any record of him	8 Feb 94	none 1920-1941
Write SS Admin.	his SS5 (application)	10 Feb 94	answer 10 April 94 ★ BINGO! birthdate + place
Write Texas Grand Lodge - Waco	his Masonic record	9 Feb 94	answer Feb 16 ★ BINGO! birthdate + place 1879-1912
Call Trinity Lutheran	Appointment to see records - looking for Grandpa baptism + m. Tom + Emilia deaths	11 Feb 94	no record found
Call 1° Evangelical Lutheran		11 Feb 94	no record of them
Call Houston Endowment	Employee records - Grandpa	11 Feb 94	Archivist has never found any employee records.
Call Missouri Synod office in Austin	Identify old Lutheran Ch. in Austin	X - found at Clayton Lib.	history of Synod in Tx No Luth. Ch. in Austin then.
Write E. Point GA archives	Grandpa WWI draft registration	20 Feb 94	no record found
Call Forest Park - Lawndale	directions to cemetery	27 Mar 94	went out there Apr 2
Call Fred	Obits for Tom + Emilia	22 Feb 94	He sent microprints 23 Feb
Call SP Railroad Personnel off. Calif.	H+TC and SP personnel records	22 Feb 94	has records only after 1980
Call Fred	Obits < Grandpa Preuss in-laws	20 Mar	found Grandpa only - sent 31 Mar
Call Annunciation Catholic Ch.	Alf + Annie m rec. 1907	11 Apr 94	no record found
Call St. Joseph Catholic Ch.	—— " ——	"	—— " ——
Call Catholic Cathedral	—— " ——	"	records in Latin, stored in boxes, weeks to search
Call Christ Church (Epis) Cathedral	—— " ——	"	no record of them
Call Joe Wells	—— " ——	wait til after tax season...	
Call John			

Example 4   UNPUZZLING YOUR PAST WORKBOOK

8

PART TWO

Forms for Organizing Research and Files—Indexes

Two kinds of indexes are provided here. First, the public records indexes facilitate the use of deed and marriage indexes and the Soundex and serve as checklists for your work. The second group indexes ancestors and various notes and handouts in your own files.

DEED INDEX FORM

The deed index form (1) provides space to record the basic information often found in town or county deed indexes and (2) saves time in transcribing it. Armed with the indexes, you are ready to read the original record books, even on microfilm. For filing in appropriate binders or folders, use a separate form for each surname in each locality.

The form matches the grantor (direct) and grantee (indirect or reverse) organization of most courthouse indexes. For example, when you search for all deeds under the surname Williamson, you may find Williamsons selling (grantors) as well as buying (grantees). Thus, on the form that shows "Grantor" in the first column, you will record all Williamson sellers in that locale during your chosen time period. The back of the form provides space to list all Williamson buyers (grantees) from the reverse index. Example 5 illustrates the use of this form.

You will want to study not only your immediate ancestors in the deed records but also the cluster formed by their relatives, friends and neighbors. Studying the *cluster* helps you learn about your direct lineage. Relatives and neighbors often bought from and sold to each other and witnessed each other's transactions. Even if your ancestor owned no land, he could have been a witness for a neighbor who may turn out to be his brother-in-law, father-in-law or stepfather. In addition, finding an ancestor as a witness also shows he was alive on that day and may help narrow down a death date or moving date.

Refer to chapter 11 of *Unpuzzling Your Past* for explanation of various indexing systems used

for courthouse records. Consult chapter 11 in *Unpuzzling Your Past* or chapter 5 in *The Genealogist's Companion & Sourcebook* for discussion of deed records and their genealogical value.

MARRIAGE INDEX FORM

The marriage index form is organized in a similar manner. Grooms of your target surname can be listed on the front of the form; brides, on the back. The form provides space to document your notes—where you used the index and how you could find the same information again. This index information helps you locate vital statistics on direct ancestors and study the cluster of relatives in a given county or state. Example 6 illustrates the use of this form.

STATEWIDE MARRIAGE INDEX FORM

The statewide marriage index form is useful for searches in those states which have centralized marriage indexes in print, in microform, or in files in the state archives, historical society or other depository. These indexes can help you identify brides and grooms of your research surname, the town or county of record, a date (of license, marriage or filing), and sometimes a reference or other information. With this index data, you can contact the appropriate agency or institution for copies of the ones you need or perhaps rent the microfilmed records to see them for yourself and abstract any additional information they may contain.

Example 7 shows two ways that this form can be used. One option, shown at the bottom of the example, simply lists the information straight off the index. It just happens that all but one of the brides are from the same county. The groom index at the top of the example is an alternative way of organizing the information from a statewide index. Listed first are all the Cato/Cater grooms who were marrying in Monroe

County, the county being studied. Next are those from neighboring counties. Grooms from one county sometimes married in a next-door county if that was the bride's residence. Also, people by the same surname living in neighboring counties were often relatives. Grooms from the parent county (the county from which Monroe originated) were grouped next. With a less common name such as Cato/Cater, grooms living in the same area of the state need to be studied as possible relatives.

Chapter 11 of *Unpuzzling Your Past* and chapter 5 of *The Genealogist's Companion & Sourcebook* discuss marriage records and their genealogical use.

SOUNDEX SEARCH FORM

The soundex search form provides space to record the basic information from the microfilmed Soundex (or Miracode) cards. The form can be adapted to at least two kinds of searches. First is the search for all households of a given surname in a given locale, whether town, county or state, such as all Crooms in Texas in 1900. The second is a search for a particular person, whether or not a head of household. The shaded row on the form can be used to list information on that person that will help in the identification on the Soundex: name, race, age, birth place, residence, and other persons you expect to find in the same household. This shaded area keeps that information handy as you search and record households with likely candidates.

Example 8 shows two searches for specific individuals in the 1900 Soundex. The search for the first girl, Minnie, was complicated by the fact that nothing concrete was known about her as the search began, except an approximate birth date. Four possible candidates were found, but the four birth dates given in the census were all different from the date the family had been given. Thus, the search had to continue into other censuses and other documents to compile and sort out enough data to make an informed decision on which Minnie was the correct one. The second search, for Bettie May, had an exact birth date, known to be correct, and the name of a brother. Only one Bettie M. turned up on the Soundex, and she had a brother by the right name. The searcher then used other sources to verify that this was indeed the correct family, in spite of the fact that the birth date given in the census was wrong. However, it is not unusual for birth dates in the 1900 census to be off by even two or three years. (The 1900 census is the only one before

1960 that asked for month and year of birth).

The earliest Soundexed census is the 1880 census. The 1880 census covers only families listed with children ten and under, and the 1910 Soundex is not available for all states. Refer to chapter 12 and Appendix E in *Unpuzzling Your Past*, third edition, and chapter 2 in *The Genealogist's Companion & Sourcebook* for discussion of the Soundex and for 1910 Soundex availability. For your convenience, the appendix on pages 43 and 44 provides two references: a list of information reported in the federal censuses, showing which information appears in which censuses, and a review of the Soundex coding system.

ALPHABETICAL ANCESTORS CHART

The alphabetical ancestors chart can be used in a number of ways. Adapt it to your own needs. I use it in the following ways, and a blank form is provided for each:

1. As a master list for *one surname*, placed at the beginning of a notebook or file, to identify and sort out the people in that family.

2. As a finding and identifying aid for *one locality* (city, county, state or country) of ancestors from that place. This is especially handy when you visit that locale and don't want to spend valuable research time looking for someone in the wrong place or time period. Example 9 is a master list of this kind: ancestors from the state of Kentucky.

3. As a master list, *one or two alphabet letters to a page*, of all known ancestors, placed first in a notebook of family group sheets and/or pedigree charts. For example, all surnames beginning with *A* and *B* may fit on one page; all beginning with *C* may need their own page.

INDEX TO WORKSHOP NOTES AND HANDOUTS

The index to workshop notes and handouts is the only way I have found to keep up with all the pages of notes and handouts from seminars, in such a way that I can refer to them and benefit from them long after the event itself. Some people file these notes and handouts in file folders or half-inch binders, one for each occasion. Others put them in that "someday stack" of "papers I don't know what to do with right now but will get around to later." After trying the latter method unsuccessfully for some years, I sorted them all into large three-ring binders and then needed a way to find specific information easily. This index has worked well for me.

All-day seminars usually deal with several topics, each of which needs to be listed in the index. I find that I need to look up information by topic more often than by the lecturer's name, so I file all items from one seminar or speaker together in the notebook and index alphabetically by topic. The index refers me to the speaker who presented that topic. (See Example 10.) When one binder is full, I add another. I use a notebook divider for each lecturer and arrange it alphabetically in the binder.

Regardless of how you organize, you can get the most out of a seminar only when you *do* organize. Speakers often put much time and effort into preparing useful topics and handouts, and audiences seldom go away empty-handed. All this effort is fruitless if we never look at the notes and handouts again. This index can fix the problem!

An alternative form for indexing workshop notes and handouts is provided for those who already have or hope to have many such entries and prefer to designate their own alphabetical headings on the columns of the form. With this form, you can use one letter of the alphabet for each column and use multiple pages, or create any other division that fits your need.

Deed Index—Grantors

Deed Index for __Caddo Parish__ County __LA__ State Surname __CROOM__

Source: Courthouse or Library __Caddo Parish Courthouse, Shreveport__ Call #, Film # __—__

Grantor Surname: CROOM	Grantee	Book, Page	Date	# Acres	Type Transaction or Legal Description
Isaac "	T. Mooring	H-488	1853	land	S2 T19 R16
Isaac "	Calvin S. Croom	donation A-14	1853	240 A	S2 T19 R16
C. S. "	James Christian	H-540		land	S2 T19 R16
Isaac "	" "	L-194	1857		S1 T19 R16
Isaac "	Jno A. Bickham	L-656	1858		slaves - sale
C. S. "	" " "	M-422	1859	67½ A	S19 T20 R15
" " "	Saml Gerald	N 598	1860	land	S19+20 T20 R15
John "	Benj. B. Bonham	P 15	1866	land	S30 T20 R15
Isaac "	Louisa C. Harris	P 975	1868	donation	S29+30 T20 R15
Calvin S. "	Methodist Ch. S.	V 442	1875	¼ A	S25 +36 T20 R15

Deed Index—Grantees

Deed Index for __Caddo Parish__ County __LA__ State Surname __CROOM__

Source: Courthouse or Library __Caddo Parish Courthouse, Shreveport__ Call #, Film # __—__

Grantee Surname: CROOM	Grantor	Book, Page	Date	# Acres	Type Transaction or Legal Description
Isaac "	Jos. Allen	C 225	1844		NW¼ S2 T19 R16
" "	Jos. R. Belton	C 227	1844		NE¼ S2 T19 R16
" "	Timothy Mooring	H 478	1853		W½ NW¼ S1 T19 R16
" "	Thos. Philyan etux.	L 248	1857		
C. S. "	T. Mooring	T 45	1873		power of attorney
" " "	Jno + Lou Harris	X 459	1879		
Calvin S. "	Timothy Mooring Sr.	N 267	1860		
" " "	" " Tutor	N 279	1860		
Wm H. B. "	Heirs of CS + MA Croom	18 - 700	1897		various

Example 5   UNPUZZLING YOUR PAST WORKBOOK

12

Marriage Index—Grooms

Marriage Index for **CADDO PARISH** (County) **LA** (State) Surname **CROOM**

Source: Courthouse or Library **parish courthouse, Shreveport** — Call #, Film # _____

Groom	Bride	Date	Book, Page	#
Calvin S. Croom	Margaret A. Mooring	12 Jan 1851	1 - 262	
Isaac Croom	Mrs. Elizabeth Robinson (sic)	22 June 1846	1 - 143	bond
H. H. B. Croom	Bennie Lindsay	22 Nov 1905	30 - 541	
Isaac Croom Jr	Ann Maria Robertson	16 May 1856	1 - 484	license
Isaac Croom	Maria Ann Robertson	15 Sept 1856	2 - 10	solemnized

Marriage Index—Brides

Marriage Index for **CADDO PARISH** (County) **LA** (State) Surname **CROOM**

Source: Courthouse or Library **parish courthouse, Shreveport** — Call #, Film # _____

Bride	Groom	Date	Book, Page	#
Isabella Croom	Jno. Bland	18 Aug 1846	1 - 111 / 1 - 102	
Lucille M. "	Andrew J. Brewer	14 Jan 1909	34 - 507	
F. C. "	Thos. Cooper	20 Aug 1884	15 - 181	
Roberta "	R. M. Hales	1 Nov 1883	14 - 694	
Elvira "	R. Kelly	11 Jan 1847	1 - 138	
Elvira "	Roderick Kelly	15 Jan 1848	1 - 147	
Piety "	Robt. D. Packer	30 July 1850	1 - 213	bond
Eliza "	D. H. Powell	3 Oct 1877	10 - 191	
Irene Margaret "	Jas. Taylor Hood	2 Oct 1889	18 - 121	
Nina E "	S. O. Williams	23 Nov 1910	36 - 245	

Statewide Marriage Index for ___AL___ Surname _Cato/Cater_

State   Soundex Code

Source of this information: _Early Alabama Marriages 1813-1850_ (Call #,) Film # _Gen.976.1 E12 ALA_
(San Antonio: Family Adventures, 1991) Vol.3C   _Clayton Library_

Groom		Bride	Date	County	Reference
A. J.	Cato	Sarah G. McPherson	20 Dec 1865	Monroe	None given
Alex J.	"	Elizabeth East	8 Feb 1865	Monroe	"
Elbert W.	"	Sabrina Ann Booker	10 July 1840	Monroe	"
Lamenthurn W.	"	Catherine Rawls	6 May 1834	Monroe	"
William	Cater	Margaret A. Sigler	5 Aug 1858	Monroe	"
neighboring counties					
William	Cato	Emeline Maness	31 Oct 1831	Wilcox	"
William D.	Cater	Marinda Powell	11 July 1839	Wilcox	"
parent county					
B. P.	Cato	Lottie Moore	22 July 1828	Washington	"

Statewide Marriage Index for ___NC___ Surname _Shelby_

State   Soundex Code

Source of this information: _1977 microfiche, NC State Archives_ ___ Call #, Film # _card 35_
(also gives bondsmen & witness-see notes)   _at Clayton-C52D5_   _bond #_

Bride		Groom	Date	County	Reference
Betsy	Shelby	Jacob Clonts	16 Feb 1815	016-01-043 Cabarrus	7457
Dorcas	"	Wm. Alexander Kerr	9 Feb 1807	065-01-130 Mecklenberg	82032
Harriett	"	Alanson Alexander	17 Dec 1823	065-01-002	79985
		bondsman Milton Shelby			
Isabella	"	Stephen Alexander	22 Nov 1797	065-01-007	80080
Marg^t J.	"	Wm. Marshal	m.16 June 1864	065-01-160	82537
Susan Cornelia	"	John T. Harry	m. 25 Mar 1858	065-01-098	81524
Sarah	"	John Alexander	15 Aug 1798	065-01-005	80050
Susanah	"	Dan Alexander	11 June 1800	065-01-003	80004
(At Clayton, finding aids notebook has list of county codes)					
065 = Mecklenberg Co.					

Example 7

Soundex Search for **BLALOCK**   B 442   Year _1900_   State _TN_

Surname   Code

Given Name or Head of Household	Color & Age	Birth-place & Citizen.	County	City, Street Address	Vol, E.D., Sheet, Line	Other Family Members or Enumerated With
Search for: *Minnie Blalock*	WF c16 "b May 1884 I think"	TN	*nothing more known at time of search—* (*Minnie is sometimes a nickname for Mary.*)			
	Date from an old aunt who knew her	*1900 census gave month + year of birth, but not always correctly.*				*Knowing siblings' names could be a great help—*
James T. Blalock	W Sept 1860	TN	*Lincoln*		ed 62 sheet 28 line 18	*wife Mary + Geo 1880, Clara 1882, Minnie Feb 1884 Clayton 1886 all b TN*
John Blalock	W Mar 1861	TN	*Putnam*	*Not enough data here to determine who is correct girl. Gather more info on these + subject.*	ed 68 sheet 5 line 13	*wife Louisa Ann Charlie 1885 Minnie 1887 Maggie 1890 Bertha 1895 Emery 1897*
Pitser M. Blalock	W June 1845	TN	*Hardeman*		ed 145 sheet 8 line 35	*wife Catheran Loe 1877 Minnie Mar, 1885 Jesse 1889 all b TN*
Giles Blalock	W May 1858	TN	*White*	*Census ages and birthdates often are wrong.*	ed 155 sheet 8 line 46	*wife Rosie Mary Oct 1885 andy 1888 Davie 1896 allice 1898*

Soundex Search for **BLALOCK**   B 442   Year _1900_   State _TN_

Surname   Code

Given Name or Head of Household	Color & Age	Birth-place & Citizen.	County	City, Street Address	Vol, E.D., Sheet, Line	Other Family Members or Enumerated With
Search for: *Bettie May Blalock*	Known b 11 July 1885 age 14-15	TN	(*Bettie is sometimes a nickname for Elizabeth.*)			*Had brother Jesse Dee*
Edward Blalock	W M Feb 1869	TN	*White*		ed 154 sheet 2 line 62	*wife Nancy Elizzie Oct 1890 addison Lavena Earnest + Isaac* — *B-date too late*
Fannie Blalock widow	W F May 1858	TN	*Hardeman*	*New Castle*	ed 145 sheet 7 line 66	*son Trimble Apr 1877 ★son Dee Jan 1881 ★dau Bettie M May 1886* — *Right girl but wrong date*

Alphabetical Ancestors

Locality **KENTUCKY**
County and/or State

Surname or Maiden Name	Given Name	Birth Year	Death Year	Residence	Dates of Residence	5-Gen. Chart #
ALLISON	ROBERT	by 1765	1816	SHELBY Co.	by 1800 –1816	5
ALLISON	JOSEPH	c1790 –1794	1831	SHELBY Co.	by 1800– 1831	5
ALLISON (m Metcalfe)	MARY BELL	1820	1868	SHELBY Co. DAVIESS Co.	all life	1,5
JAGGERS	DANIEL		1808	HARDIN Co.	after 1800 –1808	8
LITTLER (m Metcalfe)	REBECCA	1770 –1776	after 1840	SHELBY Co.	c1802 –death	5
METCALFE	JOSEPH SR.	1765 –1770	1840	SHELBY Co.	c1802 –1840	5
METCALFE	JOSEPH JR.	1814	TX 1887	SHELBY Co. DAVIESS Co.	1814— c1877-79	5,1
METCALFE	THOMAS MOODY	1852	Tx 1930	DAVIESS Co.	1852 — c1871-76	1

Index to Workshop Notes and Handouts

Topics M–N	Lecturer	Topics O–P–Q–R	Lecturer
Military Records	Bockstruck	Ohio Research	Witcher
Migration & Settlement	Hooverson	Okla Historical Society	See Okla 1988 Boyle
" see also	Bockstruck	Old Southwest	Bockstruck
Mississippi Research	"	Organizing	Dollarhide
		"	G. Carter
New England sources	Schoeffler		
New Orleans Notarial archives	Reeves	Passenger Lists	Hansen

PART THREE

Forms for Gathering Information

Once your search is planned and organized and you get to the library, courthouse or interview session, you can work faster and more efficiently in certain searches with prepared forms. The ones provided here include a form for note taking from books, articles or documents; a form for abstracting deeds; census extraction forms; and forms to stimulate interviewing for family history.

NOTE-TAKING FORM

You may not need a prepared form for writing down notes from cemetery transcriptions or tax records or a county history. However, a form is provided for your convenience and to help in remembering the documenting process. That process is the primary caution in note taking. Ask yourself, "How can I (or someone else) find the same information again? How can I give proper credit to the source if I use this information in an article, book or family history? What evidence backs up my conclusions and data? What am I taking directly (quoting) from this source and what am I paraphrasing?" Perhaps this form will offer a not-so-subtle reminder and help establish good research habits. The form can be used for almost any book, public record or family papers. Examples 11 and 12 illustrate three of these applications.

Genealogists need to record *all* sources they consult. Usually, we don't know whether a source contains something useful until we look through it. Thus, writing down the bibliographic information *first* creates a record. We can always put in our notes: "No Shelbys in index. No mention found in chapter on King's Mountain." However, if the book or article discusses a place or event which was pertinent to the family, even if it did not refer to them by name, the text may contain useful background or details which add to your understanding of the family's experience and surroundings. Notes taken now from such a work could prove helpful later in your search.

DEED ABSTRACT FORM

Especially when genealogists begin their search, they may not have had much experience with courthouse records. Deeds are one kind of valuable public document found in courthouses (and on microfilm) and often can be abstracted more quickly with the help of a form set up much like the document itself. This form is organized to handle the most common situations found in deed records. Example 13 is an abstract of a warranty deed, often called simply a *deed*, which has considerable genealogical value.

Remember that the grantor is the seller and the grantee, the buyer. Refer to chapter 11 in *Unpuzzling Your Past* and chapter 5 in *The Genealogist's Companion & Sourcebook* for discussion of deeds and their genealogical use. The example on the research planning worksheet, page 7, illustrates genealogical gleanings from several deeds as applied to one search.

CENSUS FORMS

Many people begin their genealogical efforts with census records once they have done preparatory work in family sources. It seems there is always census work to do. Thus, one of the most widely used forms in genealogy is the census extraction form. The census forms in this book, 1790 through 1920, plus the slave schedule forms, follow the original government forms, column by column, so that note taking is easy. Remember that before 1850, only heads of household were named and members of the household were listed by sex and age groups. Beginning in 1850, every free person was listed by name. Thus, two examples are provided here, one before and one after 1850. Example 14, from 1830, demonstrates the ease of making multiple entries of the same surname since a number of families will fit on one form. The 1830 example also illustrates the value of finding every census for a given individual. If the searcher skipped the 1830 census for Abiel Fellows, what a gem he or she would miss!

Example 15, from 1880, however, holds only one family because everyone in the household is listed individually. This family is an example of a his-hers-and-ours blended family, something to keep in mind in studying censuses.

Here are a few reminders about census research:

1. Be sure to copy *everything* given in the original, as it appears in the original, including people with different surnames. Such persons may be relatives. Copy information at the top of the page, including enumeration date, and every column where something is marked. (See page 2 for a brief explanation of *census day*. See also page 64 of *Unpuzzling Your Past*, third edition, and chapter 2 in *The Genealogist's Companion & Sourcebook* for further discussion of *census day*.)

2. Read ten to twenty families on either side of yours, or the entire enumeration district or county, looking for relatives. Because the census was usually recorded in the order of visitation down a street or road, relatives living near each other often appear near each other in the census. Remember that ancestors lived, worked and worshiped within a cluster of relatives, friends and neighbors. Studying this cluster often provides clues or information on the ancestor(s) we are seeking.

3. Look for every ancestor in all available censuses taken during that lifetime.

4. Reading the Soundex or index never takes the place of reading the original. If you do not find your family-of-interest in the Soundex or index, read the entire county or enumeration district where you expect them to be at that time. If they lived in a city, use other sources such as city directories, maps and newspapers to narrow down the area in which to search.

5. Remember that people were missed in every census, and some censuses for some locations have been lost. In the case of the burned 1890 census, see *The Genealogist's Companion & Sourcebook*, page 18, for a detailed survey of the surviving fragments.

6. Chapter 2 of *The Genealogist's Companion &*

Sourcebook is an entire chapter devoted to federal census records, finding aids and supplemental schedules. See *Unpuzzling Your Past*, third edition, pages 63-66 and 75-78 for discussion of census research.

INTERVIEW FORMS

Forms for interviewing family members can help elicit information on personal and family *history*. You can gather vital statistics and basic genealogical information on family group sheets, but many of us need reminders and memory-joggers to ask pertinent questions about history as the family experienced it. The interview forms in this book are therefore organized by decade or era. The questions provided are by no means all the questions to ask. They are intended as a springboard to memories. Expand into whatever areas your interviewee takes you. Ask additional questions about how history affected the family, how and why people did the things they did, when and where events took place within the family, who had interesting experiences, what daily life was like, and the ways life is different now. Refer to chapters 7, 8 and 9 in *Unpuzzling Your Past* for more questions and suggestions for successful interviewing.

Some of the questions, such as those asking about membership in organizations and religious groups, could produce valuable answers which lead you to other sources for research. If a male interviewee says he is a Mason, for example, ask whether his father, uncles or grandfathers were also Masons. Masonic records, depending on place and time, can be helpful in locating birth, death, and residence information on men who were members. Discovering a family's religious affiliation in the early twentieth century may lead you to congregational records or cemeteries where more vital data may be found, even on previous generations.

The questions on the forms, by necessity, are general. Make them specific to your own family. Expand into other sheets of paper as needed when you get stories or lengthy answers. Encourage your interviewee to give you details and specifics. Example 16 shows a slight change in the dates covered, at the request of the interviewee, to discuss his life before his marriage.

Notes   Surname _Black (Rev. Sam)_

Title of (book,) article, or document _The Tinkling Spring: Headwater of Freedom_ # vols. in set _____

For articles, title of journal _____
    volume # _____ , issue # and date _____ , page #s _____

(Author,) compiler, and/or editor _Howard McKnight Wilson_

City of publication _Fishersville, VA_   Publisher and date of publication _Tinkling Spring & Hermitage_
Presbyterian Churches 1954

Where I used it and when _Clayton Library_ _____ date _July 1978_

Call # or Film # _975.5 W748 Va_   *Get all index references first & check off as you use them.*

Vol # (when applicable), _Index:_
Page #   Notes _Rev. Samuel Black 80-82, 151, 154, 156-7, 159, 167, 170, 176, 430-31_

| 80 | North & South Mountain congregation asking for supply preacher. located on head of "Shenandoe." Joined in the call when Donegal Presbytery 1745 voted unanimously to transport Rev. Sam Black after his acceptance & installed him as regular pastor. At first he refused to move to VA. For this disobedience, he was publicly reproved by the presbytery. |
| 81 | *quoted from the book* "After Mr. Black's unfortunate experience over the transfer to N & S Mt in 1745, he was reinstated in his old pastorate at Conewago, but was soon in trouble "4 them again." It |

Notes   *Article title in quotes*   Surname _Harrison (William)_

Title of book, (article) or document _"The Right Reverand William Harrison of_ # vols. in set ____
Revolutionary Virginia, First 'Lord Archbishop of America'"
For articles, title of journal _Historical Magazine of the Protestant Episcopal Church_
    volume # _53_ , issue # and date _1 (March 1984)_ , page #s _25-43_

Author, compiler, and/or editor _Otto Lorenz, Kearney State College, Kearney NE_

City of publication _____ Publisher and date of publication _____

Where I used it and when _Rice Univ Library_ _(UH too)_ date _Feb 1993_

Call # or Film # _BX 5800. H5_

Vol # (when applicable),
Page #   Notes

| 25 | Harrison had been chaplain to Lord Cornwallis at Gloucester, British garrison across York R from Yorktown. Harrison was rector, Bristol Parish, Dinwiddie & Prince |

Notes

Surname __SHAW__

Title of book, article, or (document) __Davidson County TN Court Minutes__ # vols. in set ____

For articles, title of journal _____

     volume # _____ , issue # and date _____ , page #s _____

Author, compiler, and/or editor _____

City of publication __Nashville__   Publisher and date of publication __Tenn. State Archives__

Where I used it and when __microfilm, rented__   date __Aug 1978__

Call # or Film # _____

Vol # (when applicable), __Vol. A (6 Oct 1783 – 15 July 1791)__

Page #	Notes
7	7 Jan 1784 - James Shaw recorded his stock mark as half crop in left ear + under kiel in right ear + brand: F2
21	July 1784 - grand jury included James Shaw.
26	July 1784 - James Shaw established ferry cross the Cumberland R at Nashville. Shaw requested "that he keep a Ferry at the place afforesaid [sic] with good + sufficient boats + well attended for the purpose of passage of such as are desirous of crossing the said river" at the following fees: 1 shilling — man + horse 1 shilling — every pack horse + pack 8 pence — lead horse without pack 6 pence — every footman 6 pence — every head of horned cattle 4 pence — every head of sheep + hogs
146	7 July 1785 - deed from Thomas Molloy to James Shaw acknowledged.
253	2 July 1787 - James Shaw is security for David Fry (?), sheriff.
282	8 Apr 1788 — James Shaw on jury. Case: State vs. Samuel Martin, accused of stealing bull from James Bosley. Defendant pleaded not guilty. Jury found him not guilty.

Example 12

Deed Abstract

Surname **BRELSFORD**

Source (Courthouse, microfilm & #, other) **Courthouse**

County or town where filed **Christian** State **KY** Deed Book # **C** Inclusive pages **137**

Quitclaim deed _____ Warranty deed **✓** Bill of sale _____ Deed of trust _____ Deed of gift _____

This indenture made this day **11 Oct** in the year **1810**

between (grantor) **Phoeby + Frances Garner, Nathan Brelsford + wife Elizabeth, 3 of the** of _____ **KY**
names(s) **heirs of Henry Garner, dec'd.** county (or town), state

[box:] This shows that Elizabeth's maiden name was Garner.

and (grantee) **Peter Dick** of **Frederick Co VA**
name(s) county (or town), state

The said grantor(s) for and in consideration of the sum of **$950** [Is it <u>dollars</u> or other currency?] paid by grantee(s)

and/or notes in the amount of _____ at _____ percent interest, due on date(s) _____,

or other considerations [describe] _____

have sold (or given, if deed of gift) to the grantee(s) the following property: **384** acres, situated in **Frederick**

county, state of **VA**, described as follows: [Copy waterway, boundaries, neighbors, whatever it says.] **beginning at double white oak on West point of a hill of the Pine Cabin Ridge, then N20E 200 poles to 2 white oaks + a locust sapplin[g] on S side near _____ of a ridge, then S60 E 320 poles to 2 pines on the top of a ridge, then S30 W 214 poles to a white oak + black oak on E side of a ridge, then N57 W 278 poles to the beginning... being land conveyed to said Henry Garner by deed of bargain + sale by Henry Garner + wife Jane, dated 6 Sept 1776 + recorded in Frederick Co. Henry Garner d intestate + these heirs are selling their portions of the estate.**

[box:] The deed should encourage the searcher to study both Henrys further.

and/or other property described as: _____

In witness whereof the grantors have set their hands and seals. [Note who signed and who made a mark instead.]
Nathan, Frances, + "Pheba" signed.
Elizabeth made her X.

Witnesses: **none listed**

[box:] This request shows that the Brelsfords + probably the sisters were living in Christian County.

Does the seller's wife relinquish her dower right? _____ When? _____

Does the seller's wife willingly sign and seal the indenture? **The Frederick Co. court asked the Christian Co. court to get answer + send to them since Elizabeth could not conveniently come to Frederick Co. to be examined.**

Date the deed is acknowledged in court _____ Date recorded _____
[See Frederick Co records for Elizabeth's answer + recording date.]

Example 13

1830 or 1840 Census—Part 1

Local Community __TOWNSHIP OF BRADY__   County __ST. JOSEPH__   State __MICHIGAN__

Enumerator __ELIAS TAYLOR__

Date Census Taken __12 Nov 1830__   Enumerator District # ____

[Official census day—1 June 1830-1840]   Supervisor District # ____

Written Page No.	Printed Page No.	Name of Head of Family	Free White Persons (including heads of families)																							
			Males											Females												
			under 5	5-10	10-15	15-20	20-30	30-40	40-50	50-60	60-70	70-80	80-90	90-100	100 & over	under 5	5-10	10-15	15-20	20-30	30-40	40-50	50-60	60-70	70-80	80-90	90-100	100 & over
	180	Abiel Fellows	0	2	0	3	0	0	0	0	1					1	1	3	0	0	0	1					
	181	James Fellows	0	0	0	0	1									0	0	0	1								

Census taker added this note : "This man is sixty five [years] of age has nineteen living children ten of which is under his care was a soldier in the Revolution is a man of Sober habits of unusual enterprise and great strenght [sic] of mind has never received any thing from our government for his Early and Youthful strugle [sic] for Independence is it to [sic] late to hope ??"

19 children minus 10 at home leaves 9 to well be this one.

other Fellows in Michigan—all in Wayne County outside of Detroit.

20	Festus A. Fellows	0	0	0	0	1									1	0	0	0	1								
20	Rice L. Fellows	1	0	0	0	0	1								1	0	0	0	1								
22	James Fellows	0	0	0	0	0	0	1							0	0	0	2	0	0	1						
22	Albert H. Fellows	2	0	0	2	1									0	0	0	0	1								

Gathering the others in the state, especially when there are only a few, will help in studying a family. These 4 Fellows are likely to be related to each other + may be related to Abiel.

Example 14

1880 Census

Local Community __Precinct 8__ County __Williamson__ State __TX__ roll #1333
Enumerator __H. A. Highsmith__ (county is split on 2 rolls)
Date Census Taken __23+24 June 1880__ Supervisor District # __5__
[Official census day—1 June 1880] Enumerator District # __162__

Written Page No.	Printed Page No.	Street Name	House Number	Dwelling Number	Family Number	Name of every person whose place of abode on 1 June 1880 was in this family (3)	Color (4)	Sex (5)	Age (6)	Month born if during census year (7)	Relationship to head of this household (8)	Single (9)	Married (10)	Widowed / Divorced (11)	Married during year (12)	Profession, Occupation or Trade (13)	Months unemployed this year (14)	Currently ill? If so, specify. (15)	Blind (16)	Deaf & dumb (17)	Idiotic (18)	Insane (19)	Disabled (20)	School this year (21)	Cannot read (22)	Cannot write (23)	Birthplace (24)	Birthplace of Father (25)	Birthplace of Mother (26)
53	583			1	459	J.E. Tisdale	W	M	51							farmer											AL	AL	AL
				1	459	Sallie Jr "	W	F	40		wife		1			keeps house											TN	TN	NC
						Bland Harris [sic]	W	M	18		son-step	1				works on farm											TX	VA	TN
						Mattie E Harrison	W	F	16		step-dau	1				at home											"	"	"
						Wm L. Harrison	W	M	14		step-son	1				"								1			"	"	"
						Sigar [sic] Tisdale	W	F	13		dau	1				"								1			"	AL	"
						Sterling O. Tisdale	W	M	6		son	1				"								1			"	AL	"
						Benjamin S Tisdale	W	M	4		son	1				"											"	blank	"
						Sterling Argain	W	M	44		bro-law	1				works on farm											TN	VA	TN

Sallie's kids by first husband! Bland was also a Harrison.

These 3 are JE's kids, but only the 2 boys are also Sallie's. Other sources show that JE + Sallie had been married 9 years in 1880.

This is the census first first to ask for relationships.

Sterling + Sallie siblings. This is not NC(?) not passed on to all other evidence...TN; This should be TN.

Example 15

Pre-1930 Period

Interview with **RAY LODEN**

Interviewer, date, place __EAC, 13 Jan 1996, his home, Houston Tx__

He asked to keep interview pre-1925. He and Ruby married in 1925 + just celebrated 70th anniversary!

Your age in ~~1930~~ 1925 _____ or circle as appropriate: child   teenager   (young adult)   adult

Size of your family in the 1920s: __9__. Names of persons in the household & relationship to you:
Father + mother, 4 brothers + 2 sisters. Details on attached page.

Residence(s) before ~~1930~~ 1925, with dates, street, town, state __farm near Wills Point Tx, Route 1__
made calls through operator. Were on rural party line. Their ring was 3 longs and a short.

When did the family get any of these "modern conveniences"? Telephone __1918__ Car __1915__ Electricity __none__

Indoor plumbing __none__ Running water in the house __none__ Vacuum cleaner __none__ Electric fans __none__

Washing machine __none__ Other?

What kind of cooking stove did you or your mother use before 1930? What kind of refrigeration for food? **Wood-burning stove. Ice box for refrigeration. Had no well, but had brick-lined + concrete cistern. Lowered syrup buckets full of buttermilk into cistern to keep milk cool.**

How was your house heated in the winter? **fireplaces + wood heater. First had kerosene lamps for light, then Coleman lights (gasoline).**

Did your family own its home? __yes__ Rent? _____ How much was rent? _____

What can you tell me about your house(s) before 1930? Rooms? __6__ Size? (One) two or more stories? (Wood) brick, etc.? **House had dogtrot through middle: Living room (doubled as bedroom), 1 bedroom, dining room, kitchen on 1 side; 2 bedrooms on other side. Fireplace in 2 rooms. Smokehouse.**

Did your family ever experience a house fire? __no__ flood? __no__ other natural disaster? __no__ Elaborate.
Had storm cellar but few occasions to use it.

Were you a student before ~~1930~~ 1925? __yes__ How far in school did you go? __through college__

How far from home was your school? __1¼ mi from rural school-grades 1-10.__ 10 miles from high school-last year (11th grade) he boarded in town. School went only to 11th grade then.

Did you have to buy your books or did the school provide them? __bought books__

What can you tell me about your elementary or high school experiences?
drama, debate, athletics - basketball + tennis

What jobs did family members hold in the 1920s or before? (Did any of the women work outside the home?) __No.__
farming.

Did you work in the 1920s? Doing what? **On farm. (had cattle tanks + ponds for water)**

How did you decide "what you wanted to be when you grew up"? (Methodist minister) Was conscious of a spiritual call. Had encouragement from Christian parents + a loyal pastor.

What did you do for entertainment in the 1920s or before? **hunting, fishing, basketball** made their own crystal set. Could get 1 Dallas station. Loved to hear Hawaiian music.

When did you or your family get a radio for the first time? __1922__ a phonograph? __none__

Did anyone in the family play a musical instrument? Who? What? **Brother George + sister Mildred played piano.**

How often did you go to movies? Favorites? **Maybe once a year. Westerns were his favorites.**

Example 16

Did the family have pets? Explain. a dog to work cattle, cats to control rodent population

What part did sports or games play in your life in this period? entertainment - basketball, tennis, marbles + keeps, sometimes mumblety peg.

During childhood, what is your earliest memory of home and family? How old were you? 4 years old. Father was seriously injured working on railroad. Had to be hospitalized - which was rare. Births + illnesses usually treated at home. This experience made him realize there were hospitals + what they were.

What is your earliest memory of events outside the family? How old were you? same

During childhood, what were your favorite toys and games? Did you make any of your own toys? made stick horses, go-carts, + play wagons.

To what extent were family gatherings part of your life before 1930? Explain.

To what extent were religious activities a part in your life before 1930? 1925 Explain. Religious activities were as essential as good conduct + honesty in the home.

What, if any, rules governed Sunday or the Sabbath in your home before 1930? 1925 (1) No manual labor except feeding the livestock. (2) No cooking - baking was done on Saturday. (3) No athletic games or picture shows, except croquet - because his father loved to play croquet.

Was dancing allowed in your family? no Card playing? no Dating without a chaperone? no
Were family members restricted in what they could read for pleasure? yes. Mother or dad would read it first to approve or disapprove.
What other rules or customs governed behavior?

How did your family celebrate or observe birthdays? Christmas or other religious holidays? July 4?
Special days were celebrated with friends, family + loved ones.

What wedding or funeral customs do you remember in your family or community in this period? Weddings were conducted in the home or at church. Brides wore what they had or got a dress they could use again - not usually white.

Do you remember when you or your family got a camera for the first time? 1921

What kind of transportation did you use most? wagon, buggy, car after 1915

How did you get to school or work? walked to rural school for 10 grades. Boarded in town for last year of high school.

What did the family do at lunch time? Come home or eat elsewhere? What do you remember about school lunches? All meals were eaten at home. School lunches were carried in lunch pail or syrup bucket. Took syrup in quinine bottle - held enough syrup for 2 biscuits.

Was the main meal at noon or in the evening? What did you call that meal? main meal at noon, called it dinner.

If you lived on a farm, what crops did the family raise? What food? Crop - cotton. Food - wheat (exchanged for barrel of flour), corn (went to grist mill on Saturdays), oats, fruit orchard, vegetables, hogs, beef, + chickens.

Did any family members serve in the military in World War I? Who? Where? Brother George Dee was in student army officers group, could continue school + get training. Was still training at end of war.

How did the family celebrate the end of World War I? They celebrated in every way they could make noise.

Was this a good period in your life? yes How did your experiences before 1930 affect your life thereafter?

Example 16 Cont'd.

PART FOUR

Forms for Reference and Study

This group of forms provides an organized way of recording and storing information already known to be true or accepted as a result of careful evaluation of data. The forms capsule a search so that you can see how much you know about a given person or family and where there are holes in your information. They give you "the big picture" and help you view your progress in ways that will surprise you. Using these forms can be an extremely valuable exercise.

FAMILY GROUP SHEET

The family group sheet is one of the most universally used and valuable forms for genealogists. It contains vital information on one nuclear family, i.e., parents and their children. As I study a family in depth, I create a group sheet for every ancestral couple and separate forms for each of their children and each of their brothers and sisters. For example, if great-grandpa was one of six siblings, I make a separate sheet for each of his brothers and sisters. If great-grandpa and great-grandma had four children, I make a separate form for each of the four, including the one who was my own grandparent. Why? Because ancestors did not live in a vacuum, but in a cluster of friends, neighbors and relatives. By studying the cluster in which these ancestors lived, worked and worshiped, we not only get a better picture of their lives and times but may learn more about them than we could by studying only the ancestral couple itself. Group sheets of the extended family show us important parts of the cluster, generation by generation, and identify many of the names we find in the same documents with our own ancestors.

Many versions of family group sheets are available. I prefer one that reads vertically like most other papers in a notebook and one that has writing space big enough that I don't have to use a magnifying glass to read what is there. This particular group sheet format has served me well. It can display vital information as well as the sources which provided the details. With each person on the chart, list the source number(s) applicable to that person, and list the references on the back. Please refer to chapter 3 of *Unpuzzling Your Past* for further discussion of these charts.

Example 17 is one of my own families. The group sheet has gone through a number of versions over the years as I have added data about my family. It is to a point now where I can add new sources as I find them without having to retype the whole form. This format was especially useful in making me answer very basic questions: How do I know Thomas was the son of William and probably the son of Elizabeth? How do I know Catey was the daughter of Isaac? How do I know Elizabeth Steele was Isaac's wife (actually, his first wife) and Catey's mother? (Some researchers list only his second wife as if she were the only one). How do I know Steele was her maiden name? How do I know all of these children were really children of Thomas and Catey? And on and on. Although the census records before 1850 do not name the children living at home, they at least account for the children who were supposed to be in the family in each of those years. Thus, I listed those census reports in the sources, and they support the other data. They also place the family in a given location in those years.

AHNENTAFEL TABLE

The ahnentafel table is a concise way of listing the ancestry of any one person and assigning a standard identification number to each ancestor. (*Ahnentafel* is a German word meaning *ancestor table* or *family tree*.) Many pedigree charts, such as the five-generation chart on page 33, employ these numbers for the most recent four or five generations (numbers 1-31). Then, when you begin a new chart to add more generations of ancestors, you begin with the same numbers 1-31 again. However, many genealogists find it logical and helpful to continue the ahnentafel numbering beyond the first chart (most recent 31 people) to the more remote generations. The ahnentafel chart in this book is a reference for seven generations. The reader is invited to extend the list as necessary beyond that point.

Calculating the ahnentafel number for any person

is very easy. Double any person's number to identify the father. Double the number and add one to identify the mother. For example, if you want to prepare your own pedigree on the table, begin with yourself as number one. Doubling *one* to *two* gives your father's number; doubling that to *four* gives his father. Doubling your own number and adding one gives 2 + 1 = 3, which is your mother's number. Thus, the parents of ancestor number twelve would be twenty-four and twenty-five. You can carry the system as far back as you find ancestors.

Using this chart helps you see readily where the holes are and may spur you on to tackle the search for the more elusive ancestors. Because these numbers can get a little unwieldy in long lists, I prefer to divide them into paternal and maternal halves. Besides, we usually think of ancestors by the "side" to which they belong. Dividing them into the two halves may help us keep them straight. Example 18 shows one page of the ahnentafel table.

FIVE-GENERATION CHART

The five-generation chart, also called a pedigree chart, illustrates one person with four generations of ancestors: parents, grandparents, great-grandparents and great-great-grandparents. Each vertical column represents one generation. This chart gives you a different viewpoint from the family group sheets, which (1) detail two generations, (2) include siblings, and (3) can go forward as well as back in time. In contrast, the five-generation chart allows you to evaluate the generations, especially for proper dates and places, by viewing several generations at once. If you use this form for information that you have already proved or accepted as true based on evidence, you may not need to list documentation on the back since you would have the sources documented elsewhere on your family group sheets and in your notes and files. However, if you feel you need a reminder of where you found each piece of data, you can list sources for each person on the back of the chart. If you have not used this kind of form before, see chapter 3 of *Unpuzzling Your Past* for instructions.

Example 19 represents an in-progress search which has hit some "brick walls," one due to adoption. Nevertheless, the search goes on, gathering evidence which is yielding data for family group sheets and biographical outlines even where vital statistics for the five-generation chart are still wanting.

FIVE-GENERATION AHNENTAFEL CHART

The five-generation ahnentafel chart is for those searchers who want to extend their ahnentafel numbers to the five-generation charts so that each ancestor has one consistent identification number. On this form, you supply your own numbers from your ahnentafel table. Example 20 illustrates the process.

BIOGRAPHICAL OUTLINE

The biographical outline can be a working record of your progress in studying a particular ancestor, or it can be used for a more-or-less finished presentation. By listing specific events in the life of the ancestor as you find them in records and documents, you can study the person with greater perception than by having the events scattered in isolated documents throughout a file or notebook. Listing the events chronologically allows you to evaluate your findings: to relate events to each other, to see cause and effect, to discover patterns, to identify migrations, to review dates for conflicts or inconsistencies, to find holes in your research, to identify new places and sources to search, and perhaps even to enjoy the fruits of your search! Recording the documentation for each piece of information encourages you (1) to research carefully and thoroughly, (2) to use more primary sources than secondary ones, and (3) to question yourself: How do I *know* this date is correct? How do I *know* the list of children is accurate? How do I know the event took place *here*? How do I *know* the maiden name?

If we rely heavily on published (or unpublished) family and county histories for our information, we probably will accumulate little real evidence to back up our conclusions. Why? Few family and county histories, for many reasons, are thorough in their documentation of details. The most reliable evidence that we genealogists find usually comes from such sources as contemporary family Bibles, deeds and land records, wills and probate files, public marriage records, church records, tax rolls, military records, some census records and some newspapers. Dozens of sources exist in public records as well as in family papers. Mistakes can be found in nearly any kind of source, but the sources that are closer in time to the original event and those involving eyewitnesses or firsthand accounts are usually more reliable.

The outline can include whatever you choose and be as detailed as you want to make it. It is more interesting and more useful with a thorough coverage of whatever you find on the subject: birth, marriage, death, birth of children, military service, land transactions, court appearances, professional or occupational events, religious milestones, participation in community affairs, etc. In mentioning these events on the outline, some searchers list only a brief "headline" entry, knowing the details are in notebooks or files. Other genealogists want more explanation, comment or clarification in the outline. The example provided here leans on the side of more comment.

Example 21 is from a search that has accumulated more than will fit into two pages. Only the first two of its pages are used here. Additional records and information are still being sought to answer questions which arise from studying the data collected so far: What is the earliest evidence of Sterling in Tennessee? Is there any evidence of Sterling himself in Virginia? What evidence may narrow down the dates of his moves from county to county in Tennessee and his move to Texas?

UNITED STATES MAP

Studying maps in relation to genealogy can help us see the effects of geography on the life and decisions of a family. They may lead us to study migration routes and patterns and can aid in our understanding of how history affected the family. Maps are visual reminders of where the family was during the lives of its members and during wars, natural disasters and events of national importance. Sometimes, we even discover that ancestors in different parts of the family were at one time neighbors. In other words, maps are very useful tools for genealogists. In fact, every genealogist needs a good atlas and a good historical atlas of the United States, and any other country from which you study ancestors.

As you determine the migrations within each ancestral family, you can plot the various migrations and residences on a map such as the one provided in this book. One map may show migrations of several lines before they became joined by marriage in one county or town. Or you may choose to show only the male members of one surname on each map. Use it as it fits your needs and to illustrate what you want to show.

Example 22 depicts two Southern families who followed very different migration routes over several generations until certain members ended up together along the Texas gulf coast in the late nineteenth century. Because of space limitations on the map itself, a key is provided to detail each stop along their way.

TIMELINE

As you study ancestors and try to fit them into appropriate surroundings, circumstances and events, a timeline may prove useful as well as interesting. Such a device also allows comparison of one ancestor's life with the lives of other relatives. Where do they overlap? Who was alive during "the war"? Who lived longest? Who lived through both the American Revolution and the Civil War? What may have prompted the family to move over the mountains or down the valley when they did? What events in the "old country" may have caused the family's immigration to America?

The purpose of the chart is to remind us that our ancestors lived not in a vacuum but in a time and place surrounded by other people. They lived through the history we once studied in school and may have forgotten. We sometimes need to be reminded of that history. For example, we need not spend time trying to find Pennsylvania records from the 1650s because that colony was not settled until 1682. Sometimes a visual representation is the best way to keep such things in perspective.

Although timelines such as those provided here cannot list all pertinent events, they can include certain key events to trigger further investigation into ancestors' lives and times. The two timelines included in this book cover the periods 1600 to 1800 and 1750 to 1950, overlapping a little so that fewer ancestors have to be split between charts. The solid lines divide the charts into segments of twenty-five years each. Place the ancestors with their life dates on the chart any way you choose. It may be helpful to include the ahnentafel numbers of the ancestors charted.

As with the military records checklist, you can limit each form to one surname or use it as a master chart for all ancestors who lived in the same period. (Example 23 is a master chart with ancestors from both the paternal and maternal lines.) Be creative and use it as it suits you.

Family Group Sheet of the ___Thomas Patton___ Family

	Source #			Source #
Thomas Patton	1	Birth date	4 Feb 1794	3
Full name of husband		Birth place	SC, possibly York Co.	4
William Patton	4	Death date	24 April 1852	3, 2
His father		Death place	Fayette Co, TN	32
Elizabeth	4	Burial place	Rehobeth Cemetery, Fayette Co (Presbyterian church gone)	31
His mother with maiden name				
Catherine Ewing McFadden	1, 3, 24	Birth date	22 Jan 1798	3
Full maiden name of wife		Birth place	SC, probably Chester Co.	1
Isaac McFadden	1	Death date	30 Mar 1873	3
Her father		Death place	probably Hardeman Co, TN	9, 10
Elizabeth Steele	22	Burial place		
Her mother with maiden name				

Other Spouses none	Marriage date, place, etc. 4 July 1816, in SC, probably Chester or York Co.
Source #s	Source #s 3

Listed in birth order, using full names.

Children of this marriage	Birth date & place	Death date, place, & burial place	Marriage date, place & spouse
1. William Ewing Patton Source #s 3, 5, 6, 7, 11, 13	22 Nov 1817 SC possibly York Co.	14 Jan 1897 Senatobia, Tate Co, MS	28 Jan 1840 Fayette Co, TN Agnes Abigail Kerr/Karr
2. Sarah Jane Patton Source #s 3, 5, 6, 7, 9, 10, 12	18 Sept 1819 SC possibly York Co.	Apr 1885	John L. Day
3. James McFadden Patton Source #s 3, 6, 7, 13, 14, 16, 29	1 Aug 1824 SC probably York Co.	3 May 1870 Fayette Co, TN Mt Pleasant Cem, Hickory Withe	19 Jan 1848 Fayette Co, TN Emily Narcissa Kerr/Karr
4. Elizabeth Olevia Patton Source #s 3, 6, 7, 17	18 Dec 1825 SC probably York Co.	Feb 1887	before 1850 Allen P. Gilliam
5. Isaac Steele Patton Source #s 3, 6, 7, 18, 19	11 Dec 1827 (1826?) SC probably York Co.		13 Sept 1848 Fayette Co, TN Mary A. Dickson
6. Margaret Catherine Patton Source #s 3, 6, 7, 9, 10, 20, 21, 23, 33	25 Feb 1829 (Bible record) Tombstone–1828. SC prob. York Co.	19 June 1901 Brown Co, TX Zephyr Cem.	12 Oct 1847 Fayette Co, TN Elliott Glen Coleman

Discrepancy in b-date for #6 creates possible question on b-date for #5. Must study both.

Example 17

Source #   Sources (Documentation)

1   Probate records, Chester Co, SC, Bk K, Folios 123-126, SC Archives.
Isaac McFadden estate records show Thomas Patton as heir (in right of wife). Return of debts and accounts of estate of Isaac McFadden, 19 Mar 1829, showing 4 payments to Thomas Patton "on legacy." Isaac and family lived in Chester Co. as shown in many deeds and church records:

1b   <u>Early Records of Fishing Creek Presbyterian Church, Chester County, South Carolina, 1799-1859</u>, Brent H. Holcomb and Elmer O. Parker, compilers, Bowie, MD: Heritage Books, 1991, facsimile reprint of original records.

2   Letter from "Catherin M. Coleman" (dau of Thomas Patton) to brother-in-law Aurrelious F. Coleman, 18 May 1852, giving her father's death date. Copy in possession of Emily Croom. Original in possession of Thyrza McCollum, Greenville MS, until her death, June 1995.

3   Turner Coleman Bible, copied 5 May 1971, by his son Word Coleman. Bible then in possession of Word's sister Norma Irene McGary of Mullin, TX.

4   Will of William Patton, blacksmith, 30 May 1795, York Co, SC Wills, Bk 1, p 173 and case #61, file #2806, Will Bk A-12, p 139, guardianship proceedings. A few other SC Patton families had sons named Thomas, but various factors help rule out those as ours. Wife Elizabeth named in will.

5   US Census of 1820, York Co, SC, p 158A (Thomas Patton family)
6   US Census of 1830, York Co, SC, p 338   "   "   "
7   US Census of 1840, Fayette Co, TN, Dist 15, p 164 "   "
8   US Census of 1850, Fayette Co, TN, Dist 13, p 749 "   "
9   US Census of 1860, Hardeman Co, TN, p 73 (Catey Patton, Day, Coleman)
10   US Census of 1870, Hardeman Co, TN, Dist 3, p 139 (Catey Patton, Coleman)

11   Fayette Co, TN, Marriage Bk A, p 32 (William E Patton)
12   US Census of 1850, Fayette Co, TN, p 242 (Wr p 482) (John & Sarah Day)
13   Letters from Rachel & Leslie Karr Patton, grandson of Wm E Patton, to Emily Croom, 2 Jan 1981, 4 June 1971, with Wm E Patton info and 30 Mar 1974 with dates of James McF Patton from cemetery.

pr p = printed page #
wr p = written page #

14   US Census of 1860, Fayette Co, TN, Dist 7, p 101-102 (James McF Patton)
15   Fayette Co, TN, Marriage Bk A, p 152 (James M. Patton)
16   Letters and chart from Lily McElroy Harrison, g-granddau of James & Emily Patton, to Emily Croom, about 1978 (not dated).

17   US Census of 1850, Fayette Co, TN, Dist 4, wr pg 528, pr pg 264B, family #445. Gilliam. No indication whether any of the children are Elizabeth's.

18   Fayette Co, TN, Marriage Bk A, p 161 (Isaac S. Patton)
19   US Census of 1850, Fayette Co, TN, wr pg 499, pr pg 250. Isaac S Patton. Have not found this family after this.

20   Fayette Co, TN, Marriage Bk A, p 143 (Patton-Coleman)

21   US Census of 1850, Hardeman Co, TN, family #222, pr p 84, wr p 167 (Coleman)

22a Jones Co, NC, Deeds, Bk G, p 154-155, names Elizabeth <u>Steele</u> as wife of Isaac McFadden, 1790. Chester Co, SC, Deeds, Bk B, p 85, dated 10 June 1789, names Elizabeth as his wife, without maiden name.

22b Elizabeth d 26 June 1802, age 39. <u>Tombstone Records of Chester County, SC</u>, Louise Kelly Crowder, comp. Chester, SC, 1970, Vol 1, p 45.

23   US Census of 1880, Ganzales Co, TX, e.d. 72, pr p 376 (Coleman)
24   Fayette Co, TN, Marriage Bk A, p 238 (Patton-Day)
25   US Census of 1860, Fayette Co, TN, Dist 2, p 37 (Day)
26   US Census of 1870, Fayette Co, TN, Dist 1, p 25 (Day)
27   Fayette Co, TN, County Court Minute Book E, p 23, guardianship of 3 youngest children and support for widow.

Example 17 Cont'd.   UNPUZZLING YOUR PAST WORKBOOK
30

Family Group Sheet of the ___Thomas Patton___ Family, continued

Father ___Thomas Patton___   Mother ___Catherine Ewing McFadden___

Children of this marriage	Birth date & place	Death date, place, & burial place	Marriage date, place & spouse
7. Mary Susan Patton "deaf and dumb" Source #s 3, 7, 8, 9, 10, 27, 28	2 Mar 1834 TN probably Fayette Co	30 Mar 1873 Hardeman Co TN	never married
8. Frances Stephanie Patton Source #s 3, 7, 8, 24, 25, 26, 27, 30	8 Aug 1835 TN probably Fayette Co	2 May 1857 Fayette Co TN Somerville Cemetery	7 Dec 1853 Fayette Co TN Wiley G. Day
9. Margaritta Clementine Steadman (Steadovan) Patton Source #s 3, 8, 9, 10, 27, 28, 29	31 Oct 1840 TN probably Fayette Co	20 Oct 1869 Hardeman Co TN	Trowill
Source #s			

Source #   Sources (Documentation)

28   Bolivar, TN, Presbyterian Church Register from copy made by Louise J. McAnulty, 1969, and copied by Emily Croom, 1972. Gives membership dates of Mary and Margaritta L (sic) Patton. Beside Margaritta's name is the note "dead" without date. No indication that she had any name but Patton.

29   US Census of 1870, Mortality Schedule, TN, is missing, according to reference librarian at TN State Library and Archives, who said it apparently left the National Archives to go to Duke University (NC) but never arrived there. The other 3 mortality schedules are available.

30   Somerville Cemetery, Somerville, Fayette Co, TN, tombstones. Visited and copied by Emily Croom, July, 1973.

31   Letter from Mrs. W.L. Cargill to Emily Croom, 18 May 1993, giving burial place of Thomas Patton. Also confirmed that he left no will.

32   Fayette Co, TN, Inventory Bk H, p 66, Thomas Patton estate, 1854. My copy from TN State Archives.

33   Tombstone of Catherine Patton Coleman, Zephyr Cemetery, Brown Co, TX, visited, copied, rubbing made, by Emily Croom, Easter, 1971.

Example 17 Cont'd.

Ahnentafel Table for No. 1 _Emily Croom_

Double a person's number to find the father. Double the number and add 1 to find the mother.

Paternal Line	Maternal Line
Parents	
2 Pitzer Blalock Croom	3 Fletcher Metcalfe
Grandparents	
4 Albert Sidney J. Croom	6 Hunter Orgain Metcalfe
5 Emily Louise Blalock	7 Fletcher Elizabeth McKennon
Great-Grandparents	
8 Isaac Croom "Jr"	12 Thomas Moody Metcalfe
9 Ann Maria Robertson	13 Martha Emma Harrison
10 Pitzer Miller Blalock	14 John Fletcher McKennon
11 Mary Catherine Coleman	15 Margaret Richardson Mood
Great-Great-Grandparents	
16 Charles Croom Jr.	24 Joseph Metcalfe
17 Sivil / Sybil ?	25 Mary Bell Allison
18 Robertson	26 William Lucius Harrison
19 Elizabeth C.	27 Sarah F. Orgain
20 Jesse Blalock	28 Rev. William Richard McKennon
21 Rosanna Lea	29 Martha Elizabeth McBride
22 Elliott Glen Coleman	30 Rev. Francis Asbury Mood
23 Margaret Catherine Patton	31 Susan William Ann Richardson Logan
Great-Great-Great-Grandparents	
32 Charles Croom Sr.	48 Joseph Metcalfe
33 Temperance	49 Rebecca Littler
34	50 Joseph Allison
35	51 Mary (Polly)
36 Robertson	52 George Washington Harrison
37	53 Margaret Emma Bland
38	54 Rev. Sterling Orgain
39	55 Mary Elizabeth Jones
40 William Blalock	56 George Garner McKennon
41 Mary Cash	57 Nancy Liles
42	58 John McBride
43	59 Mary "Polly" Jaggers
44 Ferdinand Glen Coleman	60 Rev. John Mood
45 Elizabeth A. Phillips	61 Catherine McFarlane
46 Thomas Patton	62 Thomas Muldrup Logan, MD.
47 Catherine Ewing McFadden	63 Susan William Ann Richardson

Example 18

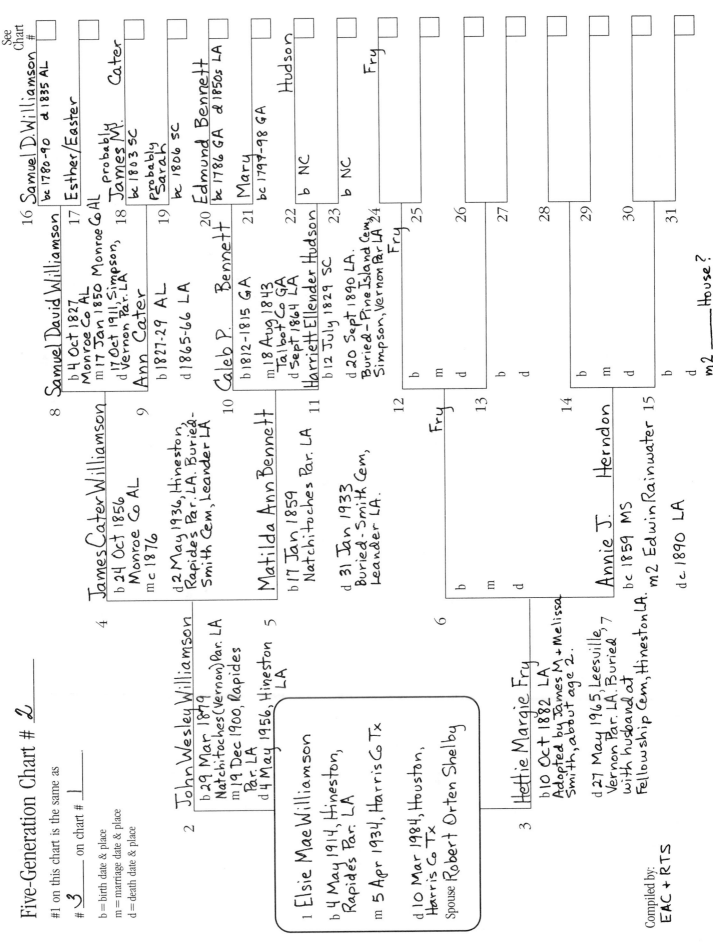

Five-Generation Chart # 2 _____

#1 on this chart is the same as

3 _____ on chart # 1 ____

b = birth date & place
m = marriage date & place
d = death date & place

16 Samuel D. Williamson
bc 1780-90   d 1835 AL

17 Esther/Easter

18 James M. Cater
probably
bc 1803 SC

19 probably Sarah
bc 1806 SC

20 Edmund Bennett
bc 1786 GA d 1850s LA

21 Mary
bc 1797-98 GA

22 Hudson
b NC

23 b NC

24 Fry

25 Fry
b
m
d

26
b
m
d

27
b
d

28
b
m
d

29

30 Herndon

31
b
d
m2 _____ House?

8 Samuel David Williamson
b 4 Oct 1827 Monroe Co AL
m 17 Jan 1850 Monroe Co AL
d 17 Oct 1911, Simpson, Vernon Par. LA

9 Ann Cater
b 1827-29 AL
d 1865-66 LA

10 Caleb P. Bennett
b 1812-1815 GA
m 18 Aug 1843 Talbot Co GA
d Sept 1864 LA

11 Harriett Ellender Hudson
b 12 July 1829 SC
d 20 Sept 1890 LA.
Buried - Pine Island Cem,
Simpson, Vernon Par. LA

12
b
m Fry
d

13
b
d

14
Herndon
b
m
d

15 m2 Edwin Rainwater
dc 1890 LA

4 James Cater Williamson
b 24 Oct 1856 Monroe Co AL
mc 1876
d 2 May 1936, Hineston,
Rapides Par. LA. Buried -
Smith Cem, Leander LA

5 Matilda Ann Bennett
b 17 Jan 1859 Natchitoches Par. LA
d 31 Jan 1933
Buried - Smith Cem,
Leander LA.

6
b
m
d

7 Annie J. Herndon
bc 1859 MS
m2 Edwin Rainwater

2 John Wesley Williamson
b 29 Mar 1879 Natchitoches (Vernon) Par. LA
m 19 Dec 1900, Rapides Par. LA
d 4 May 1956, Hineston LA

3 Hattie Margie Fry
b 10 Oct 1882 LA
Adopted by James M + Melissa Smith, about age 2.
d 27 May 1965, Leesville, Vernon Par. LA. Buried
with husband at Fellowship Cem, Hineston LA.

1 Elsie Mae Williamson
b 4 May 1914, Hineston, Rapides Par. LA
m 5 Apr 1934, Harris Co Tx
d 10 Mar 1984, Houston, Harris Co Tx
Spouse Robert Orten Shelby

Compiled by:
EAC + RTS

Example 19

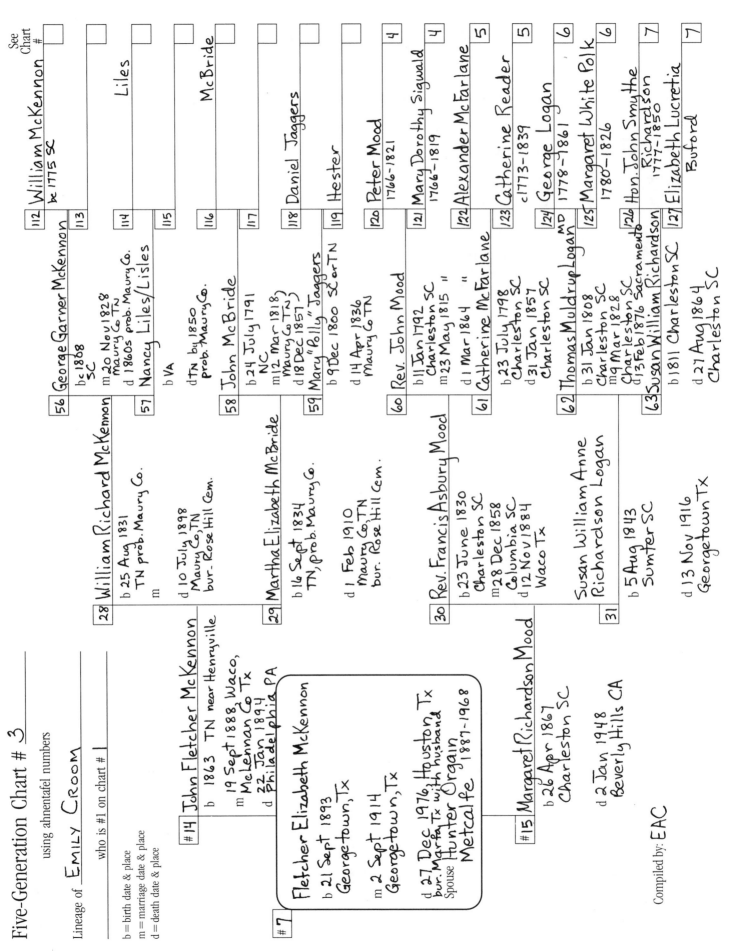

Five-Generation Chart # 3

using ahnentafel numbers

Lineage of __EMILY CROOM__

who is #1 on chart # 1

b = birth date & place
m = marriage date & place
d = death date & place

#7 Fletcher Elizabeth McKennon
b 21 Sept 1893
Georgetown, Tx

m 2 Sept 1914
Georgetown, Tx

d 27 Dec 1976, Houston Tx
bur. Marfa Tx with husband
Spouse Hunter Orgain
Metcalfe 1887-1968

#14 John Fletcher McKennon
b 1863 TN near Henryville
m 19 Sept 1888 Waco,
McLennan Co Tx
d 22 Jan 1899
Philadelphia, PA

#15 Margaret Richardson Mood
b 26 Apr 1867
Charleston SC
d 2 Jan 1948
Beverly Hills CA

28 William Richard McKennon
b 25 Aug 1831
TN prob. Maury Co.
m
d 10 July 1898
Maury Co, TN
bur- Rose Hill Cem.

29 Martha Elizabeth McBride
b 16 Sept 1834
TN, prob. Maury Co.
d 1 Feb 1910
Maury Co, TN
bur- Rose Hill Cem.

30 Rev. Francis Asbury Mood
b 23 June 1830
Charleston SC
m 28 Dec 1858
Columbia SC
d 12 Nov 1884
Waco Tx

31 Susan William Anne
Richardson Logan
b 5 Aug 1843
Sumter SC
d 13 Nov 1916
Georgetown Tx

56 George Garner McKennon
b c 1808
SC
m 20 Nov 1828
Maury Co TN
d 1860s prob. Maury Co.

57 Nancy Liles/Lisles
b VA
d TN by 1850
Prob. Maury Co.

58 John McBride
b 24 July 1791
NC
m 12 Mar 1818
Maury Co TN
d 18 Dec 1857

59 Mary "Polly" Jaggers
b 9 Dec 1800 SC or TN
d 14 Apr 1836
Maury Co TN

60 Rev. John Mood
b 11 Jan 1792
Charleston SC
m 23 May 1815 "
d 1 Mar 1864 "

61 Catherine McFarlane
b 23 July 1798
Charleston SC
d 31 Jan 1857
Charleston SC

62 Thomas Muldrup Logan MD
b 31 Jan 1808
Charleston SC
m 9 Mar 1828
Charleston SC
d 13 Feb 1876 Sacramento

63 Susan William Richardson
b 1811 Charleston SC
d 27 Aug 1864
Charleston SC

	See Chart #
112 William McKennon b c 1775 SC	
113	
114 Liles	
115	
116 McBride	
117	
118 Daniel Jaggers	
119 Hester	
120 Peter Mood 1766-1821	4
121 Mary Dorothy Sigwald 1766-1819	4
122 Alexander McFarlane	5
123 Catherine Reader c 1773-1839	5
124 George Logan 1778-1861	6
125 Margaret White Polk 1780-1826	6
126 Hon. John Smythe Richardson 1777-1850	7
127 Elizabeth Lucretia Buford	7

Compiled by: EAC

Example 20

Biographical Outline of the Life of ___STERLING ORGAIN Sr.___
<small>(Name of person)</small>

With information on education, military service, marriage(s), children, illnesses, religious milestones, migrations, residences, jobs, family events, land purchases, court appearances, death & burial, etc.

Date	Age	Event and Place	Documentation
Birth 31 Jan 1787		Place VA, probably Brunswick Co. Son of Wm Darby O. & possibly wife Elizabeth, named in his will.	Tombstone gives date (Shiloh Cem, Hutto, TX). Father in county records.
1782 & 1785		Father in Brunswick Co tax list	The First Census of the U.S., GPO, Wash., DC, 1908. Tax list used as substitute for 1790 census. No other Orgains in county tax lists.
		Used to show William's residence in the county before + after Sterling's birth	
15 Mar 1787	2/12	Father taxed in Brunswick for self & 6 slaves, 4 horses, 17 cattle.	The Personal Property Tax Lists for the Year 1787 for Brunswick Co, VA. Netti Schreiner-Yantis & Florene Love. Springfield, VA: Gen Bks in Print, 1987.
1799 & 1801	12, 14	Father on St Andrews Par, Bruns. Co. tax list (no 1800 census)	Personal property tax lists, Brunswick Co, St Andrews Parish, VA, microfilm from VA State Lib, at Clayton Lib, Houston.
1808	21	Would appear first time on poll tax	No taxes collected that year. . .
1809	22	Pers. property tax list, father's entry shows 2 white polls. Is the 2nd one Sterling?	Same as 1801.
26 June 1810	23	Father wrote will, naming kids, including Sterling	Brunswick Co VA Wills Bk 9:361-362
Aug 1810	23	Sterling not accounted for in father's household, tax list or census.	Tax list, same as 1801. US Census, 1810, Brunswick Co, VA, p 725.
1818	31	marries Mary Elizabeth Jones, dau Edmund Jones, Murfreesboro TN	Sterling named in Jones' will, Madison Co TN Will Bk 2:274-278. Letter from James Robert Orgain Jr, Alberta VA, 6-6-91, gives her full name & place.
17 Sept 1818	31	Sterling & Alfred Moore (bro-in-law), merchants/partners bought an a/c against US govt for $120 for blacksmith labor for 120 pr horseshoes for TN Mtd Volunteers in Seminole War, from Morris Lindsay.	List of Private Claims Brought Before the Senate, Vol 2:734-735. S.misc. doc.67(30-2)534.
c 1819	32	Son William E, born TN	All children living in 1852 named in Madison Co TN Deed Bk 18:464-465. Date suggested in 1850 census, Madison Co TN, Family #527.
1820	33	Not shown as head of family in census. Appears to be with in-laws (Edmund Jones) w/Mary & son Wm.	US Census, 1820, Rutherford Co TN, p 37
c 1820-21	33	dau Martha E born TN	suggested by 1830 census, her early 1840 marriage & birthdates of siblings. S.doc.37(17-1)59
Dec 1821-Feb 1822	35	Moore & Orgain petitioned Congress to be paid the $120 (see 1818). Petition referred to claims com. & tabled. 8 Feb, referred to claims committee, rejected by Treas. Dept. on grounds that volunteer gunmen got 40¢/day for use of horses & should pay own expenses for horseshoes.	
8 Feb 1822			S.doc.34(18-1)90, document B, and S.misc.doc.67(30-2)534, Vol 2:734-735.

Date	Age	Event and Place	Documentation
1822-1823	c35	Son Edmund Jones O, born TN	US Census, 1850, Madison Co TN, p 654 suggests date & gives state. S.doc. 34(18-1)90
12 Feb 1824	37	Moore/Orgain petition referred to mil. affairs committee, approved, reported out as bill #47, passed in May. Said they couldn't imagine that the Act of Jan 1795, under which volunteers were called out & pd, intended soldiers to pay for shoeing own horses during service to country. $120 had been approved by unit & regiment colonels.	
May 1824			
24 May 1824	37	Father's will probated, Brunswick Co VA	Brunswick Co VA Will Bk 9:361-362.
c 1824-25	c37	Son James born TN	Date suggested in US Census, 1850, Madison Co TN, p 654.
1825	38	Taxed for 1 poll, wife Mary taxed for 3 slaves	Madison Co TN tax roll, 1825.
1825-1826	38-39	As minister of Methodist Episcopal Church South performed weddings	Madison Co TN marriage records, various dates.
10 Nov 1825	38	Assigned power of attorney to Alfred Moore	Madison Co TN Court Minute Bk II, p 11.
Feb, May 1826	39	Hands assigned to road work	Madison Co TN Court Minute Bk II, 31, 85.
1826	39	Taxed for 1 poll, 3 slaves	Madison Co TN tax rolls, 1826.
1828	41	Taxed for 1 poll, 4 slaves	Madison Co TN tax rolls, 1828.
Nov, 1829	42	Son John Henry b near Paris, Henry Co TN	Reminiscences of the Boys in Gray. Mamie Yeary, comp. Dayton OH: Morningside, 1986 reprint of 1912 original.
1830	43	Census: 4 sons, 4 daus, 12 slaves	US Census, 1830, Henry Co TN, p 42.
1831-32	44	Dau Jane born TN	Dates for these 2 suggested in 1850 census, Madison Co TN, p 654.
1833-34	46	Dau Emily born TN	
1834	47	Local preacher elected to deacon's orders at annual conference	History of Methodism in Tennessee. John B. M'Ferrin. Nashville, 1886, III: 441.
1834-1842	47-55	Served as Trustee, Henry Co TN	The Goodspeed History of Tennessee, Carroll, Henry, Benton cos. Southern Historical Press, 1978 reprint, p 820.
1835-36	48-49	Son Sterling Jr born TN	Date suggested consistently in 1850-60-80-1920 censuses. 1900 census gives Apr 1830, but no other evidence to support that.
c 1837	50	Father-in-law Edmund Jones dies	Will probated Feb, 1838. Madison Co TN Will Bk 2:274-278.
c 1838	51	A dau born ?, name not known, indicated in 1840 census but not shown in 1850 census.	See 1840, 1850.
11 Feb 1840	53	Dau Martha m Thos P. Hall in Henry Co TN	Henry Co TN Marriages, I (1838-1852). W.O. Inman, comp. Paris, TN, 1974.
2 Apr 1840	53	Dau Sarah W. born TN, Henry Co	Her funeral notice (1928) gives date.

(handwritten note, with arrow pointing to S.doc. entry): See The Genealogist's Companion & Sourcebook for explanation and discussion of the U.S. Serial Set.

Death 4 Jan 1878	90	Place Probably Williamson Co TX Wife Mary d 19 days later, 23 Jan 1878	Tombstone gives dates for him & wife Mary.
Burial		Place Shiloh Cem, near Hutto, Williamson Co TX	
Probate ?		Place No probate record found in Williamson Co.	

Example 21 Cont'd.

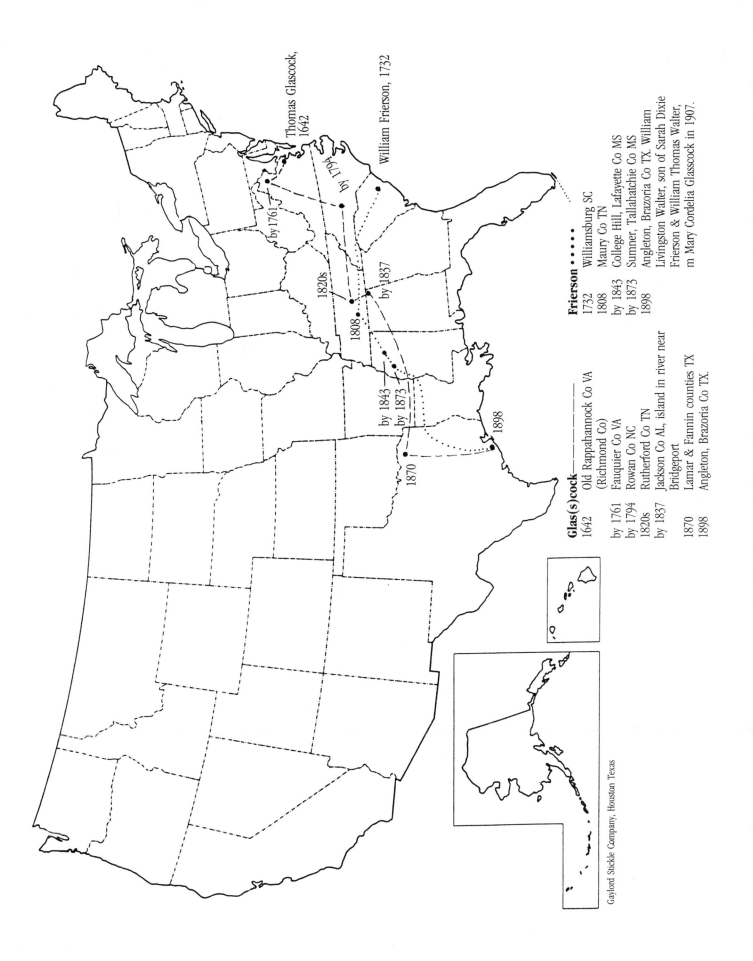

Thomas Glascock, 1642

William Frierson, 1732

by 1761

by 1794

1820s

by 1837

1808

by 1843

by 1873

1870

1898

Frierson • • • • • •
1732   Williamsburg SC
1808   Maury Co TN
by 1843   College Hill, Lafayette Co MS
by 1873   Sumner, Tallahatchie Co MS
1898   Angleton, Brazoria Co TX. William
          Livingston Walter, son of Sarah Dixie
          Frierson & William Thomas Walter,
          m Mary Cordelia Glascock in 1907.

Glas(s)cock‾‾‾‾
1642   Old Rappahannock Co VA
          (Richmond Co)
by 1761   Fauquier Co VA
by 1794   Rowan Co NC
1820s   Rutherford Co TN
by 1837   Jackson Co AL, island in river near
          Bridgeport
1870   Lamar & Fannin counties TX
1898   Angleton, Brazoria Co TX.

Example 22

Timeline 1600-1800

Family or Surname *Various, with ahnentafel numbers*

Timeline events (1600–1800):
- 1607 Jamestown VA founded
- 1620 Pilgrims land at Plymouth MA
- 1630 Massachusetts Bay Colony
- 1634 First settlers to Maryland
- 1642-1649 English Civil War
- 1649 Charles I beheaded. Cromwell & Parliament rule England.
- 1660 Restoration of established church & monarchy. Charles II crowned.
- 1670 First permanent English settlement in South Carolina
- 1682 Pennsylvania colony begins.
- 1709-1710 First large German immigration (Palatine)
- 1717 Large Scotch-Irish immigration begins, first wave.
- 1733 First settlers to Georgia
- 1754-1763 French & Indian War
- 1763 Treaty of Paris — Britain gets Canada & most land east of Mississippi River
- 1775-1783 American Revolution
- 1788 US Constitution adopted
- 1790 First US federal census

Ahnentafel #	Name	Relation	Dates
#1696	Theodorick Bland	husband	1629–1671
#1697	Anne (Bennett) Bland	wife	1639–1687
#1698	William Randolph	father	1651–1711
#849	Elizabeth (Randolph) Bland	daughter / wife	1680s–1720
#848	Richard Bland I	husband	1665–1720
#424	Richard Bland II	father	1710–1776
#425	Anne (Poythress) Bland	mother / wife	1712–1758
#506	Gabriel Guignard	husband	1708–1757
#246	Johann Peter Muth (Mood)	son / husband	1730–1778
#128	Daniel Croom	father	1680–1734-1735
#64	Jesse Croom	son	c.1713–1812

Example 23

UNPUZZLING YOUR PAST WORKBOOK

38

PART FIVE

Letter Writing

Genealogists occasionally need to write letters to agencies, institutions or individuals to request information or copies of documents. Sometimes, however, a telephone call will suffice. For example, instead of writing to the National Archives branch in East Point, Georgia, to request the form necessary for obtaining a copy of a certain World War I draft registration card, you can spend a few cents and call them at (404) 763-7477, ask that the form be mailed to you, and give them your name and address. (They have all the cards for the entire nation, not just the southeastern region. Microfilm copies are becoming available at other National Archives branches and research libraries as well.)

Likewise, if you plan to visit ancestral counties, a few telephone calls in advance can get you valuable information: the days and hours when the courthouse or library will be open, whom to contact for records of a certain church, whether the court clerks have the older records in their offices, whether some records are in storage, and whether these are accessible. This advance calling can be helpful, too, in locating certain records—finding out, for example, whether they are at the state historical society or archives, the local courthouse, or a university or public library. By telephone, you may be able to set up appointments to see certain church or funeral home records or to visit a private library that is open by appointment only. By telephone, you can learn whether a publisher or bookseller has a certain book in stock and place an order.

Instead of writing a long interview letter to a relative or friend, a telephone call or two may be easier, even if more expensive. A phone call assures you of getting an answer, and getting it quickly, and allows you to cover more thoroughly the information you want. The major concerns with such calls are whether you are able to write fast enough to take good notes as the conversation progresses and how well your interviewee hears over the telephone.

Occasionally, when your questions are specific to your research, such as pulling a given volume from library or courthouse shelves and copying the two

pages you need, you may be able to arrange the transaction by telephone. Much depends on the practice of the particular library or courthouse, how busy they are at the moment, and whether they want payment in advance.

When you do need to write letters for your research, you may have better luck if you remember the tips listed below.

LETTER WRITING TIPS FOR GENEALOGISTS

- Make the letter concise and to the point.
- Include in the letter the date, your address, and your name printed legibly. Put your return address on the envelope as well.
- Offer to pay for the service you are requesting. Most agencies which require payment will send you instructions on how they handle the fee. Many require it in advance.
- If asking for information, especially from a library, institution or government agency, generally limit yourself to one or two questions relating to one ancestor.
- When asking correspondents for information they may have on a particular ancestor, especially if the surname is common, include the ancestor's life dates and place(s) of residence for your correspondent's reference.
- Thank your correspondent in advance for the help you are requesting.
- You may want to include your phone number and suggest your correspondents call you. However, many people do not want to make long-distance calls so you may want to ask for their phone number and permission to call them.
- If writing to an individual or non-government agency or institution and expecting a reply, enclose a self-addressed *stamped* envelope (SASE). Please remember the stamp, and use the correct postage.
- Type or print your letter if at all possible. If using a computer printer or typewriter, be sure

the print is dark, sharply imprinted and easy to read. I, for one, will not answer letters that I cannot read readily.

- Proofread your letter for correct spelling and grammar, and make sure the information you give in your letter is as accurate as possible.
- You may want to keep copies of your outgoing letters so that you can have a reference when you get a response. In my early days of writing genealogy letters, I received an answer to a letter of which I had no copy. Enough time had passed that I had forgotten what I had asked. It went something like this:

Dear Emily,

In answer to your questions:

1. *Yes.*
2. *I think she did.*
3. *I have no record of it.*
4. *The fourth child was indeed Mary Louise. I remember her well. Red-headed and plump. She was just older than my mother.*
5. *I can't remember, but you might contact your Aunt Sue. She knows much of this family.*
6. *No, I don't know who she married. I think she had 2 sons and 1 daughter.*

It's good to hear from you! Good luck with your project.

When writing to relatives for information, I like to suggest that they answer *on* the letter I send them and return it to me so that I have my questions and their answers together. I leave space for answers when I type the letter. Example 24 on page 42 is this kind of letter. Sometimes public officials answer on your original letter because it is a quick way to handle correspondence. The following is one example I received years ago. Some county clerks will answer letters of this kind, and some will not. Much depends on the volume of genealogy letters they receive and the load of day-to-day business they have.

[to county clerk of Livingston County, Smithland, KY, 9 August 1978]

Dear Sir,

In working on family history, I am researching James Shaw, an early resident of Livingston County. He died there in May 1803. Do your records include a will or inventory or estate set-tlement for him? If so, please tell me the cost of obtaining a copy.

Thank you very much for your help.

Sincerely,

In searching our records, I did not find a will, inventory or settlement for a James Shaw.

[signed] James Jones, Liv. Co. Clerk

SAMPLE LETTERS

The following are a few examples of genealogy letters. Adapt the form to your own style and needs. A query letter to a journal or newspaper column needs to be concise and to the point. If the journal has a prescribed form for queries, use that. Otherwise, keep your information pertinent to your request but with enough information to let readers know whether it may be someone on whom they have information.

Query Letters

Dear Query Editor,

Seek descendants of Alexander Armstrong (c1808 MS-1872 LA) and 2nd wife Sarah Ford (c1831/33 MS-1917 LA), m 1850 in Franklin Parish LA. Issue: William A, Aaron B, Elizabeth R (m Glasscock), Margaret J (m Davidson), John, Sallie (m Lindsey), Eliza, & Robert E. Lee Armstrong, all born in LA between 1851 and 1869, probably Franklin Parish. Seek parents & siblings of wife Sarah.

Thank you for printing my query.

Sincerely,

Another kind of query letter may be sent to several families of one surname, especially in a county or town from which ancestors came, asking for information or seeking descendants. In this kind of letter, it is wise to spell out words that we genealogists often abbreviate—*born, married, died, about.*

Dear Mr. Oldham,

We are working on the genealogy of several Robertson County, TX, families and are trying to find descendants of John Charles Lafayette Oldham (born about 1856) and wife Annie (Shelby) Oldham (born about 1861, died before 1912). They married in Robertson County in 1878 and continued to live there. Their known children (born between 1879 and 1898) were Vida, John Preston, Roachal, Lycurgus (died

1973), Lula (married a Pringle), Hetty (married an Ingram), and Elam Jennings. Some of these moved to Limestone, Navarro, McLennan, and Tarrant counties. Lafayette was son of James N. and Mary W. Oldham of Robertson County. We believe Annie to be the daughter of John P. and Matilda Shelby. Lafayette had a sister Arabella Jelks, a sister M.A. McDaniel, a sister V.A. Hightower, and a brother B.F. Oldham. One grandson of Lafayette and Annie was Alvin Preston Oldham, living in Waco about 1969.

If you have information about or knew any of these Oldhams, we would appreciate hearing from you. A stamped envelope is enclosed for your convenience. Many thanks for any help you can offer.

Sincerely,

Letter Requesting Copies

One of the most common situations when genealogists need to write letters is to request a copy of a document from the institution or agency which holds it. If you know they charge a set fee for such copies, or can find out by telephone, enclosing a check for that amount may speed up an answer. Some archives, however, bill you according to the document's length. Other archives add fees for research, handling and out-of-state residents. Many will not accept partial payment in advance but want the whole fee paid before they send you the material. Therefore, you must send in a request, often on their special form (call to request one), wait for an order form to be returned to you, mail your check and wait again for your copy.

The following is an example of a letter requesting a copy of an ancestor's Social Security application, called an *SS-5*. This document often contains valuable information, such as birth date and place, parents' names, and residence and employment at the time of application.

Social Security Administration
Freedom of Information Office
4-H-8 Annex
6401 Security Blvd.
Baltimore, MD 21235

To Whom It May Concern,
In working on family history, I need to obtain

a copy of the SS-5 for this ancestor: Alfred Thomas King, SS# 467-00-0001, born about 1885–1886, possibly in Houston, Texas, and died 27 April 1941. Enclosed is a check for $7, which I understand will offset the cost of the copy. Please send it to me at the address shown above. Thank you very much.

Sincerely,

Interview Letters

Interview letters are my way of writing questions to an individual and getting the answers back on the same page. The only problem is anticipating how much space to leave for an answer. I could never judge correctly for my Great-aunt Emily, for she had much to share, and I am very grateful that she was thorough in her responses. After all, she had grown up among many of the people about whom I needed information. Sometimes, she and other correspondents have left questions blank. Expect that to happen. And remember to enclose a self-addressed stamped envelope with your request.

Example 24 is part of an interview letter dealing not with genealogical data but with historical detail that is interesting and pertinent in genealogy.

IN CLOSING

The forms provided in this book offer many options for the genealogist who wants time-saving conveniences, wants to be thorough, tries to be accurate, and makes lists or progress reports to determine how far the search has come and where it needs to go. The forms are for you to use as you wish, to adapt to your own style and needs. You may not want to use them all for every family in your search, but perhaps you will find many of them useful and will glean new ideas for planning, organizing, searching, record keeping and letter writing. Some of the forms have been adapted from those originally published in *Unpuzzling Your Past*, and others are new. All make an effort to be user-friendly.

Over the years, as I have used these, or earlier versions, I have found that they really do make a difference in how thoroughly I research, study and evaluate. I trust we all will be better genealogists as a result of this kind of effort. That is ultimately what this book is all about.

Happy Unpuzzling!

Interview Letter

Emily Croom to Emily Blalock, 4 Dec 1970

Dear Aunt Emily,
Here are some of the questions I need help with. Please answer on this page and return it to me in the enclosed envelope. Thank you so much!

1. When my granddad Albert moved to Hardeman County, did he work for the Blalocks?

    No. If my memory serves me right, he bought the farm when he married Laura Keller. Albert and Lou moved from that farm to Texas.

2. About the log house which Albert and Lou lived in. . . . Did you and Lowe move into it when Albert and Lou moved to Texas?

    Lowe bought the farm from Mr. Croom and Lou when they moved to Texas and he rented it out until we married. After our marriage in Dec. 1903, we moved into the house in January of 1904.

3. How many rooms did it have and which ones? In the picture I have, there is a window upstairs. Was that a bedroom?

    Yes. It had a big room, a kitchen, a combination bedroom and dining room, a big room upstairs over the large room downstairs, a back porch and a room over the back porch which led to the large upstairs room. The house was made of sawed logs and "chinked" as you would call it. It had a tun-and-grooved [*sic*] floor (wooden). It had been built only a few years. It had a barn, smokehouse, chicken house, as all farm houses had. There was a garden fenced with chicken-proof wire fencing to protect the vegetables. Albert and Lou were comfortably situated in every way.

4. The picture shows a lean-to addition in the back. What was it?

    A back porch with a room upstairs over the porch.

5. Did the kitchen have a fireplace or a wood stove?

    It had a very adequate large wood stove.

6. Do you remember what furniture they had in the house?

    The house was well-furnished but they had an auction sale and sold all of the furniture and took only their clothes and personal belongings with them to Texas. They went to Texas by train.

7. Were the walls on the inside covered over with wood, plaster, paper, or anything?

    The logs were sawed and chinked. Walls were as smooth as panelling is now.

8. Was the house warm in winter? cool in summer?

    Yes

9. I'd appreciate anything else you can tell me about Albert.

    I always thought of him as being a good man, and I liked him very much. He was a good neighbor. Lou and I prepared his first wife, Laura, for burial. She was sick a long time which made it very hard on Mr. Croom.

Example 24

UNPUZZLING YOUR PAST WORKBOOK

42

Federal Census, 1790-1930

WHICH CENSUS REPORTS . . . ?

age, sex, race of each individual in household	1850 forward
agricultural schedules	1850-1880
attendance in school	1850 forward
months attending school	1900
birthdate (month/year) of each person	1900
month of birth if born within the year	1870-1880
birthplace of each person	1850 forward
deaf, dumb, or blind	1830, 1850-1890, 1910
defective, dependent, delinquent schedules (DDD)	1880
pauper or convict	1850-1860
prisoner, convict, homeless child, pauper	1890
disabled: crippled, maimed, bedridden, or other disability	1880
crippled, maimed, deformed	1890
employer, self-employed, or wage earner	1910-1930
months unemployed	1880-1900
whether person worked yesterday or number on unemployment schedule	1930
home or farm as residence	1890-1910, 1930
home owned or rented	1890-1930
home owned free of mortgage	1890-1920
value of home or monthly rent	1930
farm owned or rented	1890
farm owned free of mortgage	1890
illness, current, or temporary disability	1880
chronic or acute illness, length of time afflicted	1890
immigration year	1900-1930
number of years in U.S.	1890-1900
industry/manufacturing schedules	1820, 1850-1880
insane, idiot	1850-1880
defective in mind	1890
language, native	1890, 1910-1930
native language of parents	1920
speaks English	1890-1930
male, eligible/not eligible to vote	1870
marital status	1880 forward
age at first marriage	1930
married within the [census] year	1850-1890
month of marriage, within the [census] year	1870
number of years of present marriage	1900-1910
mortality schedules	1850-1880
mother of how many children, number living	1890-1910
name of each individual in household	1850 forward
name of head of household only	1790-1840
naturalized citizen or first papers	1890-1930
year of naturalization	1920
occupation	1850 forward
parents, whether foreign-born	1870
birthplace of parents	1880 forward
radio set in home	1930
reading and writing, whether able to read or write	1890-1930
persons unable to read and/or write	1850-1880
relationship to head of household	1880 forward
slaves by age, sex	1830-1860
number of slaves	1790-1860
social statistics schedules	1850-1880
Soundex	1880 forward, mostly
street address of family	1880 forward
value of real estate owned	1850-1870
value of personal estate	1860-1870
veterans: pensioners	1840
Union vets and widows, special schedule	1890
Civil War veteran, Union or Confederate, or widow	1890
Civil War veteran, Union or Confederate	1910
veteran of U.S. military or naval forces, which war	1930

Soundex Codes

1	b, p, f, v
2	c, s, k, g, j, q, x, z
3	d, t
4	l
5	m, n
6	r

Strike out vowels and *y*, *w*, *h*. Use remaining letters for form three-digit code.
(Use initial letter of name to begin code.)
Wilhite = W430   Northway = N630

Double letters count only once.   Hill = H400   Patterson = P362

Consecutive letters in one code count once: Adcock = A322   Sumner = S560
Schmidt = S530   but Hughes = H220 (g and s are not consecutive)

Run out of letters before you get a three-digit code? Add zero.
Lee = L000   Mays = M200   Willis = W420

Get three code numbers before you finish the name? Disregard the remainder of the name.
Robertson = R163 (disregard s and n)

Census Check on _____
Name

Birthdate/place_____ First Census _____

Father's Name _____ Mother's Name _____

Marriage date/place _____ Spouse _____

Death date/place _____ Burial place _____

Census Year	Age	State/Counties Searched	County Where Found & Notes	Film #, Roll #, E.D., Pg, etc.

Census Check on _____
Name

Birthdate/place _____ First Census _____

Father's Name _____ Mother's Name _____

Marriage date/place _____ Spouse _____

Death date/place _____ Burial place _____

Census Year	Age	State/Counties Searched	County Where Found & Notes	Film #, Roll #, E.D., Pg, etc.

Census Check on _____
Name

Birthdate/place _____ First Census _____

Father's Name _____ Mother's Name _____

Marriage date/place _____ Spouse _____

Death date/place _____ Burial place _____

Census Year	Age	State/Counties Searched	County Where Found & Notes	Film #, Roll #, E.D., Pg, etc.

Census Check on _____
Name

Birthdate/place _____ First Census _____

Father's Name _____ Mother's Name _____

Marriage date/place _____ Spouse _____

Death date/place _____ Burial place _____

Census Year	Age	State/Counties Searched	County Where Found & Notes	Film #, Roll #, E.D., Pg, etc.

Census Check on _____
Name

Birthdate/place _____ First Census _____

Father's Name _____ Mother's Name _____

Marriage date/place _____ Spouse _____

Death date/place _____ Burial place _____

Census Year	Age	State/Counties Searched	County Where Found & Notes	Film #, Roll #, E.D., Pg, etc.

Military Records Checklist for _____

Ancestor Name & Life Dates	Colonial Wars (state records)	American Revolution 1775–1783 (check state & federal records)	1784-1811	War of 1812 (1812–1815)	Indian Wars 1815–1858	Patriot War 1838	Mexican War 1846–1848	Civil War 1861–1865 (for Confederates, check state & federal records)	Service 1866 forward	Spanish-American War 1898–1899	Philippine Insurrection 1899–1902	World War I 1917–1918	World War II 1941–1945

Military Records Checklist for _____

Ancestor Name & Life Dates	Colonial Wars (state records)	American Revolution 1775–1783 (check state & federal records)	1784-1811	War of 1812 (1812–1815)	Indian Wars 1815–1858	Patriot War 1838	Mexican War 1846–1848	Civil War 1861–1865 (for Confederates, check state & federal records)	Service 1866 forward	Spanish-American War 1898–1899	Philippine Insurrection 1899–1902	World War I 1917–1918	World War II 1941–1945

Research Planning Worksheet

Date _____

Statement of the Problem _____

Questions Related to the Problem:

Sources to Try	Results

Research Planning Worksheet

Date _____

Statement of the Problem _____

Questions Related to the Problem:

Sources to Try	Results

Research Planning Worksheet

Date _____

Statement of the Problem _____

Questions Related to the Problem:

Sources to Try	Results

Research Planning Worksheet

Date _____

Statement of the Problem _____

Questions Related to the Problem:

Sources to Try	Results

Contact Log # _____ Surname or Search _____

Contact plan	Subject	Contact made, date	Results & notes

Contact Log # _____ Surname or Search _____

Contact plan	Subject	Contact made, date	Results & notes

Deed Index—Grantors

Deed Index for _____ Surname _____
County   State

Source: Courthouse or Library _____ Call #, Film # _____

Grantor Surname:	Grantee	Book, Page	Date	# Acres	Type Transaction or Legal Description

Deed Index—Grantees

Deed Index for _____ Surname _____
                    County   State

Source: Courthouse or Library _____ Call #, Film # _____

Grantee Surname:	Grantor	Book, Page	Date	# Acres	Type Transaction or Legal Description

Deed Index—Grantors

Deed Index for _____ _____ Surname _____
County   State

Source: Courthouse or Library _____ Call #, Film # _____

Grantor Surname:	Grantee	Book, Page	Date	# Acres	Type Transaction or Legal Description

Deed Index—Grantees

Deed Index for _____ Surname _____
County   State

Source: Courthouse or Library _____ Call #, Film # _____

Grantee Surname:	Grantor	Book, Page	Date	# Acres	Type Transaction or Legal Description

Marriage Index—Grooms

Marriage Index for _____ _____ Surname _____
                              County   State

Source: Courthouse or Library _____ Call #, Film # _____

Groom	Bride	Date	Book, Page	#

Marriage Index—Brides

Marriage Index for _____ Surname _____
County   State

Source: Courthouse or Library _____ Call #, Film # _____

Bride	Groom	Date	Book, Page	#

Marriage Index—Grooms

Marriage Index for _____ Surname _____
County   State

Source: Courthouse or Library _____ Call #, Film # _____

Groom	Bride	Date	Book, Page	#

Marriage Index—Brides

Marriage Index for _____ Surname _____
County   State

Source: Courthouse or Library _____ Call #, Film # _____

Bride	Groom	Date	Book, Page	#

Statewide Marriage Index for _____ Surname _____

State

Soundex Code

Source of this information: _____ Call #, Film # _____

Groom	Bride	Date	County	Reference

Statewide Marriage Index for _____ Surname _____

Source of this information: _____ Call #, Film # _____

Bride	Groom	Date	County	Reference

Statewide Marriage Index for _____ Surname _____
State   Soundex Code

Source of this information: _____ Call #, Film # _____

Groom	Bride	Date	County	Reference

Statewide Marriage Index for _____ Surname _____

State

Soundex Code

Source of this information: _____ Call #, Film # _____

Bride	Groom	Date	County	Reference

Soundex Search for ＿＿＿＿＿＿＿＿＿＿＿＿＿＿＿＿ Year ＿＿＿＿ State ＿＿＿＿

Surname   Code

Given Name or Head of Household	Color & Age	Birth-place & Citizen.	County	City, Street Address	Vol, E.D., Sheet, Line	Other Family Members or Enumerated With
Search for:						

Soundex Search for _____ continued. Year _____ State _____
                    Surname   Code

Given Name or Head of Household	Color & Age	Birth-place & Citizen.	County	City, Street Address	Vol, E.D., Sheet, Line	Other Family Members or Enumerated With

Soundex Search for _____ Year _____ State _____

Given Name or Head of Household	Color & Age	Birth-place & Citizen.	County	City, Street Address	Vol, E.D., Sheet, Line	Other Family Members or Enumerated With
Search for:						

Soundex Search for _____ continued. Year _____ State _____

Surname   Code

Given Name or Head of Household	Color & Age	Birth-place & Citizen.	County	City, Street Address	Vol, E.D., Sheet, Line	Other Family Members or Enumerated With

Alphabetical Ancestors

Alphabetical Group _____
such as A-B, C-D, etc.

Surname or Maiden Name	Given Name	Birth Year	Death Year	Residence	Dates of Residence	5-Gen. Chart #

Alphabetical Ancestors

Alphabetical Group _____
such as A-B, C-D, etc.

Surname or Maiden Name	Given Name	Birth Year	Death Year	Residence	Dates of Residence	5-Gen. Chart #

Alphabetical Ancestors

Surname or Family Group _____

Surname or Maiden Name	Given Name	Birth Year	Death Year	Residence (Town, County, State)	Dates of Residence	5-Gen. Chart #

Alphabetical Ancestors, continued for Surname or Family Group _____

Surname or Maiden Name	Given Name	Birth Year	Death Year	Residence (Town, County, State)	Dates of Residence	5-Gen. Chart #

Alphabetical Ancestors

Locality _____
County and/or State

Surname or Maiden Name	Given Name	Birth Year	Death Year	Residence	Dates of Residence	5-Gen. Chart #

Alphabetical Ancestors, continued for Locality _____

Surname or Maiden Name	Given Name	Birth Year	Death Year	Residence	Dates of Residence	5-Gen. Chart #

UNPUZZLING YOUR PAST WORKBOOK

Index to Workshop Notes and Handouts

Topics A–B–C	Lecturer	Topics D–E–F	Lecturer

Topics G–H–I	Lecturer	Topics J–K–L	Lecturer

Index to Workshop Notes and Handouts

Topics M–N	Lecturer	Topics O–P–Q–R	Lecturer

Topics S–T–U	Lecturer	Topics V–W–X–Y–Z	Lecturer

Index to Workshop Notes and Handouts

Fill in alphabet headings as desired.

Topics:	Lecturer	Topics:	Lecturer

Topics:	Lecturer	Topics:	Lecturer

Notes

Surname _____

Title of book, article, or document _____ # vols. in set _____

For articles, title of journal _____

      volume # _____ , issue # and date _____ , page #s _____

Author, compiler, and/or editor _____

City of publication _____ Publisher and date of publication _____

Where I used it and when _____ date _____

Call # or Film # _____

Vol # (when applicable),
Page # _____ Notes _____

Title _____ , continued

Vol. #

Page #   Notes

Notes

Surname _____

Title of book, article, or document _____ # vols. in set _____

For articles, title of journal _____
volume # _____ , issue # and date _____ , page #s _____

Author, compiler, and/or editor _____

City of publication _____ Publisher and date of publication _____

Where I used it and when _____ date _____

Call # or Film # _____

Vol # (when applicable),
Page #   Notes

Title _____ , continued

Vol. #

Page #   Notes

Notes   Surname _____

Title of book, article, or document _____ # vols. in set _____

For articles, title of journal _____
        volume # _____ , issue # and date _____ , page #s _____

Author, compiler, and/or editor _____

City of publication _____ Publisher and date of publication _____

Where I used it and when _____ date _____

Call # or Film # _____

Vol # (when applicable),
Page #   Notes
_____

Title _____ , continued

Vol. #

Page #   Notes

Deed Abstract

Surname _____

Source (Courthouse, microfilm & #, other) _____

County or town where filed _____ State _____ Deed Book # _____ Inclusive pages _____

Quitclaim deed _____ Warranty deed _____ Bill of sale _____ Deed of trust _____ Deed of gift _____

This indenture made this day _____ in the year _____

between (grantor) _____ of _____
                         name(s)   county (or town), state

and (grantee) _____ of _____.
                        name(s)   county (or town), state

The said grantor(s) for and in consideration of the sum of _____ [Is it dollars or other currency?] paid by grantee(s)

and/or notes in the amount of _____ at _____ percent interest, due on date(s) _____,

or other considerations [describe] _____

have sold (or given, if deed of gift) to the grantee(s) the following property: _____ acres, situated in _____

county, state of _____, described as follows: [Copy waterway, boundaries, neighbors, whatever it says.]

and/or other property described as:

In witness whereof the grantors have set their hands and seals. [Note who signed and who made a mark instead.]

Witnesses: _____

Does the seller's wife relinquish her dower right? _____ When? _____

Does the seller's wife willingly sign and seal the indenture? _____

Date the deed is acknowledged in court _____ Date recorded _____

Deed Abstract

Surname _____

Source (Courthouse, microfilm & #, other) _____

County or town where filed _____ State _____ Deed Book # _____ Inclusive pages _____

Quitclaim deed _____ Warranty deed _____ Bill of sale _____ Deed of trust _____ Deed of gift _____

This indenture made this day _____ in the year _____

between (grantor) _____ of _____
                                      name(s)   county (or town), state

and (grantee) _____ of _____.
                                  name(s)   county (or town), state

The said grantor(s) for and in consideration of the sum of _____ [Is it dollars or other currency?] paid by grantee(s)

and/or notes in the amount of _____ at _____ percent interest, due on date(s) _____,

or other considerations [describe] _____

have sold (or given, if deed of gift) to the grantee(s) the following property: _____ acres, situated in _____

county, state of _____, described as follows: [Copy waterway, boundaries, neighbors, whatever it says.]

and/or other property described as:

In witness whereof the grantors have set their hands and seals. [Note who signed and who made a mark instead.]

Witnesses: _____

Does the seller's wife relinquish her dower right? _____ When? _____

Does the seller's wife willingly sign and seal the indenture? _____

Date the deed is acknowledged in court _____ Date recorded _____

Deed Abstract

Surname _____

Source (Courthouse, microfilm & #, other) _____

County or town where filed _____ State _____ Deed Book # _____ Inclusive pages _____

Quitclaim deed _____ Warranty deed _____ Bill of sale _____ Deed of trust _____ Deed of gift _____

This indenture made this day _____ in the year _____

between (grantor) _____ of _____
        name(s)   county (or town), state

and (grantee) _____ of _____.
       name(s)   county (or town), state

The said grantor(s) for and in consideration of the sum of _____ [Is it dollars or other currency?] paid by grantee(s)

and/or notes in the amount of _____ at _____ percent interest, due on date(s) _____,

or other considerations [describe] _____

have sold (or given, if deed of gift) to the grantee(s) the following property: _____ acres, situated in _____

county, state of _____, described as follows: [Copy waterway, boundaries, neighbors, whatever it says.]

and/or other property described as:

In witness whereof the grantors have set their hands and seals. [Note who signed and who made a mark instead.]

Witnesses: _____

Does the seller's wife relinquish her dower right? _____ When? _____

Does the seller's wife willingly sign and seal the indenture? _____

Date the deed is acknowledged in court _____ Date recorded _____

1790 Census

Township or Local Community —————— County —————— State ——————

Enumerator —————— Date Census Taken —————— Enumerator District # ——————

[Official census day—first Monday in August, 2 August 1790]

Page	Name of Head of Family	Free White Males 16 years & upwards including heads of families	Free White Males under 16 years	Free White Females including heads of families	All Other Free Persons	Slaves	Dwellings/ Other information

1790 Census

Township or Local Community _____ County _____ State _____

Enumerator _____ Date Census Taken _____ Enumerator District # _____

[Official census day—first Monday in August, 2 August 1790]

Page	Name of Head of Family	Free White Males 16 years & upwards including heads of families	Free White Males under 16 years	Free White Females including heads of families	All Other Free Persons	Slaves	Dwellings/ Other information

1790 Census

Township or Local Community ———————— County ———————— State ————————

Enumerator ———————— Date Census Taken ———————— Enumerator District # ————————

[Official census day—first Monday in August, 2 August 1790]

Page	Name of Head of Family	Free White Males 16 years & upwards including heads of families	Free White Males under 16 years	Free White Females including heads of families	All Other Free Persons	Slaves	Dwellings/ Other information

1790 Census

Township or Local Community ———————— County ———————— State ————————

Enumerator ———————— Date Census Taken ———————— Enumerator District # ————————

[Official census day—first Monday in August, 2 August 1790]

Page	Name of Head of Family	Free White Males 16 years & upwards including heads of families	Free White Males under 16 years	Free White Females including heads of families	All Other Free Persons	Slaves	Dwellings/ Other information

1800 or 1810 Census

Local Community ——————— County ——————— State ———————

Enumerator ——————— Date Census Taken ——————— Enumerator District # ———————

[Official census day—first Monday in August: 4 August 1800 & 6 August 1810] Supervisor District # ———————

Written Page No.	Printed Page No.	Name of Head of Family	Free White Males					Free White Females					All other free persons except Indians not taxed	Slaves
			under 10	of 10 & under 16	of 16 & under 26 including heads of families	of 26 & under 45 including heads of families	of 45 & up	under 10	of 10 & under 16	of 16 & under 26 including heads of families	of 26 & under 45 including heads of families	of 45 & up		

1800 or 1810 Census

Local Community ——————
Enumerator ——————

County ——————
Date Census Taken ——————

State ——————
Enumerator District # ——————
Supervisor District # ——————

[Official census day—first Monday in August: 4 August 1800 & 6 August 1810]

Written Page No.	Printed Page No.	Name of Head of Family	Free White Males					Free White Females					All other free persons except Indians not taxed	Slaves
			under 10	of 10 & under 16	of 16 & under 26 including heads of families	of 26 & under 45	of 45 & up	under 10	of 10 & under 16	of 16 & under 26 including heads of families	of 26 & under 45	of 45 & up		

1800 or 1810 Census

Local Community ——————
Enumerator ——————

State ——————
County ——————
Date Census Taken ——————
Enumerator District # ——————
Supervisor District # ——————

[Official census day—first Monday in August: 4 August 1800 & 6 August 1810]

Written Page No.	Printed Page No.	Name of Head of Family	Free White Males					Free White Females					All other free persons except Indians not taxed	Slaves
			under 10	of 10 & under 16	of 16 & under 26 including heads of families	of 26 & under 45	of 45 & up	under 10	of 10 & under 16	of 16 & under 26 including heads of families	of 26 & under 45	of 45 & up		

1800 or 1810 Census

Local Community _____
Enumerator _____

County _____
Date Census Taken _____
[Official census day—first Monday in August: 4 August 1800 & 6 August 1810]

State _____
Enumerator District # _____
Supervisor District # _____

Written Page No.	Printed Page No.	Name of Head of Family	Free White Males					Free White Females					All other free persons except Indians not taxed	Slaves
			under 10	of 10 & under 16	of 16 & under 26 including heads of families	of 26 & under 45 including heads of families	of 45 & up including heads of families	under 10	of 10 & under 16	of 16 & under 26 including heads of families	of 26 & under 45 including heads of families	of 45 & up including heads of families		

1820 Census

Local Community ——————

Enumerator ——————

County ——————

Date Census Taken ——————

[Official census day—7 August 1820, first Monday]

State ——————

Enumerator District # ——————

Supervisor District # ——————

Written Page No.	Printed Page No.	Name of Head of Family	Free White Males						Free White Females					Foreigners Not Naturalized	Persons engaged in Agriculture	Persons engaged in Commerce	Persons engaged in Manufacture	Free Colored Persons								All other persons	Slaves
			to 10	10 to 16	*16 to 18	16 to 26	26 to 45	45 & up	to 10	10 to 16	16 to 26	26 to 45	45 & up					Males to 14	14 to 26	26 to 45	45 & up	Females to 14	14 to 26	26 to 45	45 & up		

*Those males between 16 & 18 will all be repeated in the column of those between 16 and 26.

1820 Census

Local Community _____

Enumerator _____

County _____

Date Census Taken _____

[Official census day—7 August 1820, first Monday]

State _____

Enumerator District # _____

Supervisor District # _____

Written Page No.	Printed Page No.	Name of Head of Family	Free White Males						Free White Females						Foreigners Not Naturalized	Persons engaged in Agriculture	Persons engaged in Commerce	Persons engaged in Manufacture	Free Colored Persons										All other persons	Slaves
			to 10	10 to 16	*16 to 18	16 to 26 including heads of families	26 to 45 including heads of families	45 & up including heads of families	to 10	10 to 16	16 to 26 including heads of families	26 to 45 including heads of families	45 & up including heads of families					Males to 14	Males 14 to 26	Males 26 to 45	Males 45 & up	Females to 14	Females 14 to 26	Females 26 to 45	Females 45 & up		

*Those males between 16 & 18 will all be repeated in the column of those between 16 and 26.

1820 Census

Local Community ——————
Enumerator ——————

County ——————
Date Census Taken ——————
[Official census day—7 August 1820, first Monday]

State ——————
Enumerator District # ——————
Supervisor District # ——————

Written Page No.	Printed Page No.	Name of Head of Family	Free White Males						Free White Females						Foreigners Not Naturalized	Persons engaged in Agriculture	Persons engaged in Commerce	Persons engaged in Manufacture	Free Colored Persons											All other persons	Slaves
					including heads of families					including heads of families								Males				Females						
			to 10	10 to 16	*16 to 18	16 to 26	26 to 45	45 & up	to 10	10 to 16	16 to 26	26 to 45	45 & up					to 14	14 to 26	26 to 45	45 & up	to 14	14 to 26	26 to 45	45 & up		

*Those males between 16 & 18 will all be repeated in the column of those between 16 and 26.

1820 Census

Local Community _____

Enumerator _____

County _____

Date Census Taken _____

[Official census day—7 August 1820, first Monday]

State _____

Enumerator District # _____

Supervisor District # _____

Written Page No.	Printed Page No.	Name of Head of Family	Free White Males — to 10	Free White Males — 10 to 16	Free White Males including heads of families — *16 to 18	Free White Males including heads of families — 16 to 26	Free White Males including heads of families — 26 to 45	Free White Males including heads of families — 45 & up	Free White Females — to 10	Free White Females — 10 to 16	Free White Females including heads of families — 16 to 26	Free White Females including heads of families — 26 to 45	Free White Females including heads of families — 45 & up	Foreigners Not Naturalized	Persons engaged in Agriculture	Persons engaged in Commerce	Persons engaged in Manufacture	Free Colored Persons Males — to 14	Free Colored Persons Males — 14 to 26	Free Colored Persons Males — 26 to 45	Free Colored Persons Males — 45 & up	Free Colored Persons Females — 14 to 14	Free Colored Persons Females — 14 to 26	Free Colored Persons Females — 26 to 45	Free Colored Persons Females — 45 & up	All other persons	Slaves

*Those males between 16 & 18 will all be repeated in the column of those between 16 and 26.

1830 or 1840 Census—Part 1

Local Community _____

Enumerator _____

County _____

Date Census Taken _____

[Official census day—1 June 1830-1840]

State _____

Enumerator District # _____

Supervisor District # _____

Written Page No.	Printed Page No.	Name of Head of Family	Free White Persons (including heads of families)																														
			Males														Females																
			under 5	5-10	10-15	15-20	20-30	30-40	40-50	50-60	60-70	70-80	80-90	90-100	100 & over	under 5	5-10	10-15	15-20	20-30	30-40	40-50	50-60	60-70	70-80	80-90	90-100	100 & over				

1830 or 1840 Census—Part 1

Local Community _____

Enumerator _____

County _____

Date Census Taken _____

[Official census day—1 June 1830-1840]

State _____

Enumerator District # _____

Supervisor District # _____

Written Page No.	Printed Page No.	Name of Head of Family	Free White Persons (including heads of families)																														
			Males														Females																
			under 5	5-10	10-15	15-20	20-30	30-40	40-50	50-60	60-70	70-80	80-90	90-100	100 & over	under 5	5-10	10-15	15-20	20-30	30-40	40-50	50-60	60-70	70-80	80-90	90-100	100 & over				

7

1830 or 1840 Census—Part 1

Local Community _____

Enumerator _____

County _____

Date Census Taken _____

[Official census day—1 June 1830-1840]

State _____

Enumerator District # _____

Supervisor District # _____

Written Page No.	Printed Page No.	Name of Head of Family	Free White Persons (including heads of families)																										
			Males													Females													
			under 5	5-10	10-15	15-20	20-30	30-40	40-50	50-60	60-70	70-80	80-90	90-100	100 & over	under 5	5-10	10-15	15-20	20-30	30-40	40-50	50-60	60-70	70-80	80-90	90-100	100 & over

1830 or 1840 Census—Part 1

Local Community ——————
Enumerator ——————

County ——————
Date Census Taken ——————
[Official census day—1 June 1830-1840]

State ——————
Enumerator District # ——————
Supervisor District # ——————

Written Page No.	Printed Page No.	Name of Head of Family	Free White Persons (including heads of families)																									
			Males													Females												
			under 5	5-10	10-15	15-20	20-30	30-40	40-50	50-60	60-70	70-80	80-90	90-100	100 & over	under 5	5-10	10-15	15-20	20-30	30-40	40-50	50-60	60-70	70-80	80-90	90-100	100 & over

1830 Census—Part 2

Local Community _____

Enumerator _____

State _____

County _____

Date Census Taken _____

Enumerator District # _____

Supervisor District # _____

[Official census day—1 June 1830]

Written Page No.	Printed Page No.	Name of Head of Family (from previous page)	Slaves																					Free Colored Persons														T O T A L	White Persons included in the foregoing who are					Slaves & Colored Persons included in the foregoing who are			
			Males						Females						Males						Females							deaf & dumb under 14	deaf & dumb 14 - 25	deaf & dumb 25 & up	blind	foreigners not naturalized	deaf & dumb under 14	deaf & dumb 14 - 25	deaf & dumb 25 & up	blind
			under 10	10 - 24	24 - 36	36 - 55	55 - 100	100 & up	under 10	10 - 24	24 - 36	36 - 55	55 - 100	100 & up	under 10	10 - 24	24 - 36	36 - 55	55 - 100	100 & up	under 10	10 - 24	24 - 36	36 - 55	55 - 100	100 & up										

1830 Census—Part 2

Local Community _____

Enumerator _____

County _____

Date Census Taken _____

[Official census day—1 June 1830]

State _____

Enumerator District # _____

Supervisor District # _____

Written Page No.	Printed Page No.	Name of Head of Family (from previous page)	Slaves — Males — under 10	10 - 24	24 - 36	36 - 55	55 - 100	100 & up	Slaves — Females — under 10	10 - 24	24 - 36	36 - 55	55 - 100	100 & up	Free Colored Persons — Males — under 10	10 - 24	24 - 36	36 - 55	55 - 100	100 & up	Free Colored Persons — Females — under 10	10 - 24	24 - 36	36 - 55	55 - 100	100 & up	TOTAL	White Persons included in the foregoing who are — deaf & dumb under 14	deaf & dumb 14 - 25	deaf & dumb 25 & up	blind	foreigners not naturalized	Slaves & Colored Persons included in the foregoing who are — deaf & dumb under 14	deaf & dumb 14 - 25	deaf & dumb 25 & up	blind

UNPUZZLING YOUR PAST WORKBOOK

1830 Census—Part 2

Local Community ——————
Enumerator ——————

County ——————
Date Census Taken ——————
[Official census day—1 June 1830]

State ——————
Enumerator District # ——————
Supervisor District # ——————

Written Page No.	Printed Page No.	Name of Head of Family (from previous page)	Slaves Males under 10	10 - 24	24 - 36	36 - 55	55 - 100	100 & up	Slaves Females under 10	10 - 24	24 - 36	36 - 55	55 - 100	100 & up	Free Colored Persons Males under 10	10 - 24	24 - 36	36 - 55	55 - 100	100 & up	Free Colored Persons Females under 10	10 - 24	24 - 36	36 - 55	55 - 100	100 & up	TOTAL	White Persons included in the foregoing who are deaf & dumb under 14	deaf & dumb 14 - 25	deaf & dumb 25 & up	blind	foreigners not naturalized	Slaves & Colored Persons included in the foregoing who are deaf & dumb under 14	deaf & dumb 14 - 25	deaf & dumb 25 & up	blind

1830 Census—Part 2

Local Community _____

Enumerator _____

County _____

State _____

Date Census Taken _____

Enumerator District # _____

[Official census day—1 June 1830]

Supervisor District # _____

Written Page No.	Printed Page No.	Name of Head of Family (from previous page)	Slaves Males under 10	10-24	24-36	36-55	55-100	100 & up	Slaves Females under 10	10-24	24-36	36-55	55-100	100 & up	Free Colored Persons Males under 10	10-24	24-36	36-55	55-100	100 & up	Free Colored Persons Females under 10	10-24	24-36	36-55	55-100	100 & up	TOTAL	White Persons included in the foregoing who are deaf & dumb under 14	deaf & dumb 14-25	deaf & dumb 25 & up	blind	foreigners not naturalized	Slaves & Colored Persons included in the foregoing who are deaf & dumb under 14	deaf & dumb 14-25	deaf & dumb 25 & up	blind

1840 Census—Part 2

Local Community ——————
Enumerator ——————
State ——————
County ——————
Enumerator District # ——————
Date Census Taken ——————
Supervisor District # ——————

[Official census day—1 June 1840]

Written Page No.	Printed Page No.	Name of Head of Family (Previous Page)	Slaves — Males						Slaves — Females						Free Colored Persons — Males						Free Colored Persons — Females						TOTAL	Number of Persons employed in each family in							Revolutionary or Military Service Pensioners in the foregoing	
			under 10	10 - 24	24 - 36	36 - 55	55 - 100	100 & up	under 10	10 - 24	24 - 36	36 - 55	55 - 100	100 & up	under 10	10 - 24	24 - 36	36 - 55	55 - 100	100 & up	under 10	10 - 24	24 - 36	36 - 55	55 - 100	100 & up		Mining	Agriculture	Commerce	Manufacturing & Trades	Ocean Navigation	Canal, Lake, River Navigat'n	Learned Prof'ns & Engineers	Name	Age

1840 Census—Part 2

Local Community _____

Enumerator _____

County _____

Date Census Taken _____

[Official census day—1 June 1840]

State _____

Enumerator District # _____

Supervisor District # _____

Written Page No.	Printed Page No.	Name of Head of Family (Previous Page)	Slaves													Free Colored Persons													TOTAL	Number of Persons employed in each family in						Revolutionary or Military Service Pensioners in the foregoing	
			Males						Females						Males						Females							Mining	Agriculture	Commerce	Manufacturing & Trades	Ocean Navigation	Canal, Lake, River Navigat'n	Learned Prof'ns & Engineers	Name	Age
			under 10	10 - 24	24 - 36	36 - 55	55 - 100	100 & up	under 10	10 - 24	24 - 36	36 - 55	55 - 100	100 & up	under 10	10 - 24	24 - 36	36 - 55	55 - 100	100 & up	under 10	10 - 24	24 - 36	36 - 55	55 - 100	100 & up									

1840 Census—Part 2

Local Community ——————

Enumerator ——————

County ——————

Date Census Taken ——————

[Official census day—1 June 1840]

State ——————

Enumerator District # ——————

Supervisor District # ——————

Written Page No.	Printed Page No.	Name of Head of Family (Previous Page)	Slaves														Free Colored Persons												TOTAL	Number of Persons employed in each family in						Revolutionary or Military Service Pensioners in the foregoing	
			Males						Females						Males						Females							Mining	Agriculture	Commerce	Manufacturing & Trades	Ocean Navigation	Canal, Lake, River Navigat'n	Learned Prof'ns & Engineers	Name	Age
			under 10	10 - 24	24 - 36	36 - 55	55 - 100	100 & up	under 10	10 - 24	24 - 36	36 - 55	55 - 100	100 & up	under 10	10 - 24	24 - 36	36 - 55	55 - 100	100 & up	under 10	10 - 24	24 - 36	36 - 55	55 - 100	100 & up										

1840 Census—Part 2

Local Community ——————
Enumerator ——————

County ——————
Date Census Taken ——————
[Official census day—1 June 1840]

State ——————
Enumerator District # ——————
Supervisor District # ——————

Written Page No.	Printed Page No.	Name of Head of Family (Previous Page)	Slaves — Males						Slaves — Females						Free Colored Persons — Males						Free Colored Persons — Females						T O T A L	Number of Persons employed in each family in — Mining	Agriculture	Commerce	Manufacturing & Trades	Ocean Navigation	Canal, Lake, River Navigat'n	Learned Prof'ns & Engineers	Revolutionary or Military Service Pensioners in the foregoing — Name	Age
			under 10	10 - 24	24 - 36	36 - 55	55 - 100	100 & up	under 10	10 - 24	24 - 36	36 - 55	55 - 100	100 & up	under 10	10 - 24	24 - 36	36 - 55	55 - 100	100 & up	under 10	10 - 24	24 - 36	36 - 55	55 - 100	100 & up									

1850 Census

Post Office or Local Community ——————————— County ——————————— State ———————————

Enumerator ——————————— Date Census Taken ——————————— Enumerator District # ———————————

[Official census day—1 June 1850] Supervisor District # ———————————

Written Page No.	Printed Page No.	Dwelling in order of visitation	Family Number in order of visitation	Name of every person whose usual place of abode on 1 June 1850 was with this family	Description			Profession, Occupation, or Trade of each Male over 15	Value of of Real Estate Owned	Place of Birth naming state, territory, or country	Married within the year	In school within the year	Persons over 20 unable to read & write	If deaf & dumb, blind, insane, idiot, pauper or convict
					Age	Sex	Color							
		1	2	3	4	5	6	7	8	9	10	11	12	13

1850 Census

Post Office or Local Community ——————— County ——————— State ———————

Enumerator ——————— Date Census Taken ——————— Enumerator District # ———————

[Official census day—1 June 1850] Supervisor District # ———————

Written Page No.	Printed Page No.	Dwelling in order of visitation	Family Number in order of visitation	Name of every person whose usual place of abode on 1 June 1850 was with this family	Description			Profession, Occupation, or Trade of each Male over 15	Value of of Real Estate Owned	Place of Birth naming state, territory, or country	Married within the year	In school within the year	Persons over 20 unable to read & write	If deaf & dumb, blind, insane, idiot, pauper or convict
					Age	Sex	Color							
		1	2	3	4	5	6	7	8	9	10	11	12	13

1850 Census

Post Office or Local Community _____

Enumerator _____

County _____

Date Census Taken _____

[Official census day—1 June 1850]

State _____

Enumerator District # _____

Supervisor District # _____

Written Page No.	Printed Page No.	Dwelling in order of visitation	Family Number in order of visitation	Name of every person whose usual place of abode on 1 June 1850 was with this family	Description			Profession, Occupation, or Trade of each Male over 15	Value of Real Estate Owned	Place of Birth naming state, territory, or country	Married within the year	In school within the year	Persons over 20 unable to read & write	If deaf & dumb, blind, insane, idiot, pauper or convict
					Age	Sex	Color							
	1	2	3	4	5	6	7	8	9	10	11	12	13

1850 Census

Post Office or Local Community ———————

Enumerator ———————

County ——————— State ———————

Date Census Taken ——————— Enumerator District # ———————

[Official census day—1 June 1850] Supervisor District # ———————

Written Page No.	Printed Page No.	Dwelling in order of visitation	Family Number in order of visitation	Name of every person whose usual place of abode on 1 June 1850 was with this family	Description			Profession, Occupation, or Trade of each Male over 15	Value of of Real Estate Owned	Place of Birth naming state, territory, or country	Married within the year	In school within the year	Persons over 20 unable to read & write	If deaf & dumb, blind, insane, idiot, pauper or convict
					Age	Sex	Color							
		1	2	3	4	5	6	7	8	9	10	11	12	13

1850 Census

Post Office or Local Community ———————

Enumerator ———————

County ———————

Date Census Taken ———————

[Official census day—1 June 1850]

State ———————

Enumerator District # ———————

Supervisor District # ———————

Written Page No.	Printed Page No.	Dwelling in order of visitation	Family Number in order of visitation	Name of every person whose usual place of abode on 1 June 1850 was with this family	Description			Profession, Occupation, or Trade of each Male over 15	Value of of Real Estate Owned	Place of Birth naming state, territory, or country	Married within the year	In school within the year	Persons over 20 unable to read & write	If deaf & dumb, blind, insane, idiot, pauper or convict
					Age	Sex	Color							
		1	2	3	4	5	6	7	8	9	10	11	12	13

1860 Census

Post Office or Local Community —————

Enumerator —————

County ————— State —————

Date Census Taken ————— Enumerator District # —————

[Official census day—1 June 1860] Supervisor District # —————

Written Page No.	Printed Page No.	Dwelling Number 1	Family Number 2	Name of every person whose usual place of abode on 1 June 1860 was with this family 3	Description Age 4	Description Sex 5	Description Color 6	Profession, Occupation, or Trade of each person over 15 7	Value of Real Estate Owned 8	Value of Personal Estate Owned 9	Place of Birth naming state, territory or country 10	Married within the year 11	In school within the year 12	Persons over 20 unable to read & write 13	Deaf & dumb, blind, insane, idiotic, pauper or convict 14

1860 Census

Post Office or Local Community _____

Enumerator _____

County _____ State _____

Date Census Taken _____ Enumerator District # _____

[Official census day—1 June 1860] Supervisor District # _____

Written Page No.	Printed Page No.	Dwelling Number	Family Number	Name of every person whose usual place of abode on 1 June 1860 was with this family	Description			Profession, Occupation, or Trade of each person over 15	Value of Real Estate Owned	Value of Personal Estate Owned	Place of Birth naming state, territory or country	Married within the year	In school within the year	Persons over 20 unable to read & write	Deaf & dumb, blind, insane, idiotic, pauper or convict
					Age	Sex	Color								
		1	2	3	4	5	6	7	8	9	10	11	12	13	14

1860 Census

Post Office or Local Community —————————

Enumerator —————————

County ————————— State —————————

Date Census Taken ————————— Enumerator District # —————————

[Official census day—1 June 1860] Supervisor District # —————————

Written Page No.	Printed Page No.	Dwelling Number 1	Family Number 2	Name of every person whose usual place of abode on 1 June 1860 was with this family 3	Description			Profession, Occupation, or Trade of each person over 15 7	Value of Real Estate Owned 8	Value of Personal Estate Owned 9	Place of Birth naming state, territory or country 10	Married within the year 11	In school within the year 12	Persons over 20 unable to read & write 13	Deaf & dumb, blind, insane, idiotic, pauper or convict 14
					Age 4	Sex 5	Color 6								

1860 Census

Post Office or Local Community ———————

Enumerator ———————

County ———————

Date Census Taken ———————

[Official census day—1 June 1860]

State ———————

Enumerator District # ———————

Supervisor District # ———————

Written Page No.	Printed Page No.	Dwelling Number (1)	Family Number (2)	Name of every person whose usual place of abode on 1 June 1860 was with this family (3)	Description			Profession, Occupation, or Trade of each person over 15 (7)	Value of Real Estate Owned (8)	Value of Personal Estate Owned (9)	Place of Birth naming state, territory or country (10)	Married within the year (11)	In school within the year (12)	Persons over 20 unable to read & write (13)	Deaf & dumb, blind, insane, idiotic, pauper or convict (14)
					Age (4)	Sex (5)	Color (6)								

1860 Census

Post Office or Local Community _____

Enumerator _____

County _____

Date Census Taken _____

[Official census day—1 June 1860]

State _____

Enumerator District # _____

Supervisor District # _____

Written Page No.	Printed Page No.	Dwelling Number (1)	Family Number (2)	Name of every person whose usual place of abode on 1 June 1860 was with this family (3)	Description — Age (4)	Description — Sex (5)	Description — Color (6)	Profession, Occupation, or Trade of each person over 15 (7)	Value of Real Estate Owned (8)	Value of Personal Estate Owned (9)	Place of Birth naming state, territory or country (10)	Married within the year (11)	In school within the year (12)	Persons over 20 unable to read & write (13)	Deaf & dumb, blind, insane, idiotic, pauper or convict (14)

1850 or 1860 Census   Schedule 2—Slaves

Local Community _____

Enumerator _____

County _____   Date Census Taken _____   State _____   [Official census day—1 June]

Written Page No.	Printed Page No.	Names of Slave Owners	Number of Slaves	Description			Fugitives from the State	Number Manumitted	Deaf & dumb, blind, insane or idiotic	Number of Slave Houses	Names of Slave Owners	Number of Slaves	Description			Fugitives from the State	Number Manumitted	Deaf & dumb, blind, insane or idiotic	Number of Slave Houses
				Age	Sex	Color							Age	Sex	Color				
		1	2	3	4	5	6	7	8	9	1	2	3	4	5	6	7	8	9
		1									1								
		2									2								
		3									3								
		4									4								
		5									5								
		6									6								
		7									7								
		8									8								
		9									9								
		10									10								
		11									11								
		12									12								
		13									13								
		14									14								

1850 or 1860 Census   Schedule 2—Slaves

Local Community ————

Enumerator ————

County ———— Date Census Taken ———— State ———— [Official census day—1 June]

Written Page No.	Printed Page No.	Names of Slave Owners (1)	Number of Slaves (2)	Age (3)	Sex (4)	Color (5)	Fugitives from the State (6)	Number Manumitted (7)	Deaf & dumb, blind, insane or idiotic (8)	Number of Slave Houses (9)
		1								
		2								
		3								
		4								
		5								
		6								
		7								
		8								
		9								
		10								
		11								
		12								
		13								
		14								

Names of Slave Owners (1)	Number of Slaves (2)	Age (3)	Sex (4)	Color (5)	Fugitives from the State (6)	Number Manumitted (7)	Deaf & dumb, blind, insane or idiotic (8)	Number of Slave Houses (9)
1								
2								
3								
4								
5								
6								
7								
8								
9								
10								
11								
12								
13								
14								

1850 or 1860 Census   Schedule 2—Slaves

Local Community _____

Enumerator _____

County _____

State _____

Date Census Taken _____

[Official census day—1 June]

Written Page No.	Printed Page No.	Names of Slave Owners (1)	Number of Slaves (2)	Description			Fugitives from the State (6)	Number Manumitted (7)	Deaf & dumb, blind, insane or idiotic (8)	Number of Slave Houses (9)
				Age (3)	Sex (4)	Color (5)				
		1								
		2								
		3								
		4								
		5								
		6								
		7								
		8								
		9								
		10								
		11								
		12								
		13								
		14								

Names of Slave Owners (1)	Number of Slaves (2)	Description			Fugitives from the State (6)	Number Manumitted (7)	Deaf & dumb, blind, insane or idiotic (8)	Number of Slave Houses (9)
		Age (3)	Sex (4)	Color (5)				
1								
2								
3								
4								
5								
6								
7								
8								
9								
10								
11								
12								
13								
14								

1850 or 1860 Census   Schedule 2—Slaves

Local Community _____

Enumerator _____

County _____

Date Census Taken _____

State _____

[Official census day—1 June]

Written Page No.	Printed Page No.	Names of Slave Owners (1)	Number of Slaves (2)	Description				Fugitives from the State (6)	Number Manumitted (7)	Deaf & dumb, blind, insane or idiotic (8)	Number of Slave Houses (9)
				Age (3)	Sex (4)	Color (5)				
		1								
		2								
		3								
		4								
		5								
		6								
		7								
		8								
		9								
		10								
		11								
		12								
		13								
		14								

Names of Slave Owners (1)	Number of Slaves (2)	Description				Fugitives from the State (6)	Number Manumitted (7)	Deaf & dumb, blind, insane or idiotic (8)	Number of Slave Houses (9)
		Age (3)	Sex (4)	Color (5)				
1								
2								
3								
4								
5								
6								
7								
8								
9								
10								
11								
12								
13								
14								

1850 or 1860 Census   Schedule 2—Slaves

Local Community ———————
Enumerator ———————
County ———————
Date Census Taken ———————
State ———————
[Official census day—1 June]

Written Page No.	Printed Page No.	Names of Slave Owners (1)	Number of Slaves (2)	Description — Age (3)	Description — Sex (4)	Description — Color (5)	Fugitives from the State (6)	Number Manumitted (7)	Deaf & dumb, blind, insane or idiotic (8)	Number of Slave Houses (9)	Names of Slave Owners (1)	Number of Slaves (2)	Description — Age (3)	Description — Sex (4)	Description — Color (5)	Fugitives from the State (6)	Number Manumitted (7)	Deaf & dumb, blind, insane or idiotic (8)	Number of Slave Houses (9)
		1									1								
		2									2								
		3									3								
		4									4								
		5									5								
		6									6								
		7									7								
		8									8								
		9									9								
		10									10								
		11									11								
		12									12								
		13									13								
		14									14								

1870 Census

Local Community _____

Enumerator _____

County _____

Date Census Taken _____

[Official census day—1 June 1870]

State _____

Enumerator District # _____

Supervisor District # _____

Written Page No.	Printed Page No.	Dwelling No.	Family No.	Name of every person whose place of abode on 1 June 1870 was in this family	Description			Profession, Occupation, or Trade	Value of		Place of Birth	Parents		Month born within the year	Month married within the year	In school within the year	Cannot read	Cannot write	Deaf & dumb, blind, insane or idiotic	Males eligible to vote	Males not eligible to vote
					Age	Sex	Color		Real Estate Owned	Personal Estate Owned		Father Foreign-born	Mother Foreign-born								
		1	2	3	4	5	6	7	8	9	10	11	12	13	14	15	16	17	18	19	20

1870 Census

Local Community _____

Enumerator _____

County _____ State _____

Date Census Taken _____ Enumerator District # _____

[Official census day—1 June 1870] Supervisor District # _____

Written Page No.	Printed Page No.	Dwelling No. 1	Family No. 2	Name of every person whose place of abode on 1 June 1870 was in this family 3	Description Age 4	Sex 5	Color 6	Profession, Occupation, or Trade 7	Value of Real Estate Owned 8	Value of Personal Estate Owned 9	Place of Birth 10	Parents Father Foreign-born 11	Parents Mother Foreign-born 12	Month born within the year 13	Month married within the year 14	In school within the year 15	Cannot read 16	Cannot write 17	Deaf & dumb, blind, insane or idiotic 18	Males eligible to vote 19	Males not eligible to vote 20

1870 Census

Local Community _____

Enumerator _____

County _____

Date Census Taken _____

[Official census day—1 June 1870]

State _____

Enumerator District # _____

Supervisor District # _____

Written Page No.	Printed Page No.	Dwelling No. 1	Family No. 2	Name of every person whose place of abode on 1 June 1870 was in this family 3	Description			Profession, Occupation, or Trade 7	Value of		Place of Birth 10	Parents		Month born within the year 13	Month married within the year 14	In school within the year 15	Cannot read 16	Cannot write 17	Deaf & dumb, blind, insane or idiotic 18	Males eligible to vote 19	Males not eligible to vote 20
					Age 4	Sex 5	Color 6		Real Estate Owned 8	Personal Estate Owned 9		Father Foreign-born 11	Mother Foreign-born 12								

1870 Census

Local Community ——————
Enumerator ——————
County —————— State ——————
Date Census Taken ——————
Enumerator District #
Supervisor District #

[Official census day—1 June 1870]

Written Page No.	Printed Page No.	Dwelling No. 1	Family No. 2	Name of every person whose place of abode on 1 June 1870 was in this family 3	Age 4	Sex 5	Color 6	Profession, Occupation, or Trade 7	Real Estate Owned 8	Personal Estate Owned 9	Place of Birth 10	Father Foreign-born 11	Mother Foreign-born 12	Month born within the year 13	Month married within the year 14	In school within the year 15	Cannot read 16	Cannot write 17	Deaf & dumb, blind, insane or idiotic 18	Males eligible to vote 19	Males not eligible to vote 20

1870 Census

Local Community —————

Enumerator —————

County ————— State —————

Date Census Taken ————— Enumerator District # —————

[Official census day—1 June 1870] Supervisor District # —————

Written Page No.	Printed Page No.	Dwelling No. 1	Family No. 2	Name of every person whose place of abode on 1 June 1870 was in this family 3	Description			Profession, Occupation, or Trade 7	Value of		Place of Birth 10	Parents		Month born within the year 13	Month married within the year 14	In school within the year 15	Cannot read 16	Cannot write 17	Deaf & dumb, blind, insane or idiotic 18	Males eligible to vote 19	Males not eligible to vote 20
					Age 4	Sex 5	Color 6		Real Estate Owned 8	Personal Estate Owned 9		Father Foreign-born 11	Mother Foreign-born 12								

1880 Census

Local Community _____

Enumerator _____

County _____

Date Census Taken _____

[Official census day—1 June 1880]

State _____

Supervisor District # _____

Enumerator District # _____

Written Page No.	Printed Page No.	Street Name	House Number	Dwelling Number 1	Family Number 2	Name of every person whose place of abode on 1 June 1880 was in this family 3	Description			Month born if during census year 7	Relationship to head of this household 8	Single 9	Married 10	Widowed / Divorced 11	Married during year 12	Profession, Occupation or Trade 13	Months unemployed this year 14	Health							School this year 21	Cannot read 22	Cannot write 23	Birthplace 24	Birthplace of Father 25	Birthplace of Mother 26
							Color 4	Sex 5	Age 6									Currently ill? If so, specify. 15	Blind 16	Deaf & dumb 17	Idiotic 18	Insane 19	Disabled 20						

1880 Census

Local Community _____

Enumerator _____

County _____

Date Census Taken _____

[Official census day—1 June 1880]

State _____

Supervisor District # _____

Enumerator District # _____

Written Page No.	Printed Page No.	Street Name	House Number	Dwelling Number 1	Family Number 2	Name of every person whose place of abode on 1 June 1880 was in this family 3	Description — Color 4	Sex 5	Age 6	Month born if during census year 7	Relationship to head of this household 8	Single 9	Married 10	Widowed / Divorced 11	Married during year 12	Profession, Occupation or Trade 13	Months unemployed this year 14	Currently ill? If so, specify. 15	Health — Blind 16	Deaf & dumb 17	Idiotic 18	Insane 19	Disabled 20	School this year 21	Cannot read 22	Cannot write 23	Birthplace 24	Birthplace of Father 25	Birthplace of Mother 26

1880 Census

Local Community ——————

Enumerator ——————

County ——————

Date Census Taken ——————

[Official census day—1 June 1880]

State ——————

Supervisor District # ——————

Enumerator District # ——————

Written Page No.	Printed Page No.	Street Name	House Number	1 Dwelling Number	2 Family Number	3 Name of every person whose place of abode on 1 June 1880 was in this family	Description			7 Month born if during census year	8 Relationship to head of this household	9 Single	10 Married	11 Widowed / Divorced	12 Married during year	13 Profession, Occupation or Trade	14 Months unemployed this year	15 Currently ill? If so, specify.	Health					21 School this year	22 Cannot read	23 Cannot write	24 Birthplace	25 Birthplace of Father	26 Birthplace of Mother
							4 Color	5 Sex	6 Age										16 Blind	17 Deaf & dumb	18 Idiotic	19 Insane	20 Disabled						

1880 Census

Local Community ——————

Enumerator ——————

County ——————

Date Census Taken ——————

[Official census day—1 June 1880]

State ——————

Supervisor District # ——————

Enumerator District # ——————

Written Page No.	Printed Page No.	Street Name	House Number	Dwelling Number 1	Family Number 2	Name of every person whose place of abode on 1 June 1880 was in this family 3	Description Color 4	Sex 5	Age 6	Month born if during census year 7	Relationship to head of this household 8	Single 9	Married 10	Widowed / Divorced 11	Married during year 12	Profession, Occupation or Trade 13	Months unemployed this year 14	Health Currently ill? If so, specify. 15	Blind 16	Deaf & dumb 17	Idiotic 18	Insane 19	Disabled 20	School this year 21	Cannot read 22	Cannot write 23	Birthplace 24	Birthplace of Father 25	Birthplace of Mother 26

1880 Census

Local Community ——————
Enumerator ——————

County ——————
Date Census Taken ——————
[Official census day—1 June 1880]

State ——————
Supervisor District # ——————
Enumerator District # ——————

Written Page No.	Printed Page No.	Street Name	House Number	Dwelling Number (1)	Family Number (2)	Name of every person whose place of abode on 1 June 1880 was in this family (3)	Description			Month born if during census year (7)	Relationship to head of this household (8)	Single (9)	Married (10)	Widowed / Divorced (11)	Married during year (12)	Profession, Occupation or Trade (13)	Months unemployed this year (14)	Currently ill? If so, specify. (15)	Health					School this year (21)	Cannot read (22)	Cannot write (23)	Birthplace (24)	Birthplace of Father (25)	Birthplace of Mother (26)
							Color (4)	Sex (5)	Age (6)										Blind (16)	Deaf & dumb (17)	Idiotic (18)	Insane (19)	Disabled (20)						

1900 Census

Local Community —————

Ward —————

Enumerator —————

————— County —————

————— State —————

Supervisor District # —————

Enumeration District # —————

[Official census day—1 June 1900]

Date Census Taken —————

	Written Page No.	Printed Page No.	Street	House Number	Dwelling Number (1)	Family Number (2)	Name of every person whose place of abode on 1 June 1900 was in this family (3)	Relationship to head of family (4)	Color (5)	Sex (6)	Birth Date Month / Year (7)	Age (8)	Marital status (9)	# Years married (10)	Mother of how many children? (11)	# of these children living (12)	Birthplace of This Person (13)	This Person's Father (14)	This Person's Mother (15)	Year of Immigration (16)	# Years in U.S. (17)	Naturalized Citizen (18)	Occupation of every person 10 & older (19)	# months not employed (20)	# months in school (21)	Can read (22)	Can write (23)	Speaks English (24)	Owned or rented (25)	Owned free of mortgage (26)	Farm or house (27)	No. of farm schedule (28)

1900 Census

Local Community ——————

Ward ——————

Enumerator ——————

County ——————— State ———————

Supervisor District # ———————

Enumeration District # ———————

[Official census day—1 June 1900]

Date Census Taken ———————

Written Page No.	Printed Page No.	Street	House Number	Dwelling Number (1)	Family Number (2)	Name of every person whose place of abode on 1 June 1900 was in this family (3)	Relationship to head of family (4)	Color (5)	Sex (6)	Birth Date Month (7)	Birth Date Year (7)	Age (8)	Marital status (9)	# Years married (10)	Mother of how many children? (11)	# of these children living (12)	Birthplace of This Person (13)	Birthplace of This Person's Father (14)	Birthplace of This Person's Mother (15)	Year of Immigration (16)	# Years in U.S. (17)	Naturalized Citizen (18)	Occupation of every person 10 & older (19)	# months not employed (20)	# months in school (21)	Can read (22)	Can write (23)	Speaks English (24)	Owned or rented (25)	Owned free of mortgage (26)	Farm or house (27)	No. of farm schedule (28)

1900 Census

Local Community _____

Ward _____

Enumerator _____

County _____

[Official census day—1 June 1900]

Date Census Taken _____

State _____

Supervisor District # _____

Enumeration District # _____

Written Page No.	Printed Page No.	Street	House Number	Dwelling Number (1)	Family Number (2)	Name of every person whose place of abode on 1 June 1900 was in this family (3)	Relationship to head of family (4)	Color (5)	Sex (6)	Birth Date Month / Year (7)	Age (8)	Marital status (9)	# Years married (10)	Mother of how many children? (11)	# of these children living (12)	Birthplace of This Person (13)	Birthplace of This Person's Father (14)	Birthplace of This Person's Mother (15)	Year of Immigration (16)	# Years in U.S. (17)	Naturalized Citizen (18)	Occupation of every person 10 & older (19)	# months not employed (20)	# months in school (21)	Can read (22)	Can write (23)	Speaks English (24)	Owned or rented (25)	Owned free of mortgage (26)	Farm or house (27)	No. of farm schedule (28)

1900 Census

Local Community ———————
Ward ———————
Enumerator ———————

County ———————
[Official census day—1 June 1900]
Date Census Taken ———————

State ———————
Supervisor District # ———————
Enumeration District # ———————

	Street	House Number	Dwelling Number 1	Family Number 2	Name of every person whose place of abode on 1 June 1900 was in this family 3	Relationship to head of family 4	Color 5	Sex 6	Birth Date Month / Year 7	Age 8	Marital status 9	# Years married 10	Mother of how many children? 11	# of these children living 12	Birthplace of This Person 13	This Person's Father 14	This Person's Mother 15	Year of Immigration 16	# Years in U.S. 17	Naturalized Citizen 18	Occupation of every person 10 & older 19	# months not employed 20	# months in school 21	Can read 22	Can write 23	Speaks English 24	Owned or rented 25	Owned free of mortgage 26	Farm or house 27	No. of farm schedule 28
Written Page No. / Printed Page No.																														

1900 Census

Local Community _____

Ward _____

Enumerator _____

County _____ State _____

Supervisor District # _____

[Official census day—1 June 1900]

Date Census Taken _____

Enumeration District # _____

Written Page No.	Printed Page No.	Street	House Number	Dwelling Number	Family Number	Name of every person whose place of abode on 1 June 1900 was in this family	Relationship to head of family	Color	Sex	Birth Date		Age	Marital status	# Years married	Mother of how many children?	# of these children living	Birthplace of			Year of Immigration	# Years in U.S.	Naturalized Citizen	Occupation		Education				Owned or rented	Owned free of mortgage	Farm or house	No. of farm schedule
				1	2	3	4	5	6	Month / Year 7		8	9	10	11	12	This Person 13	This Person's Father 14	This Person's Mother 15	16	17	18	Occupation of every person 10 & older 19	# months not employed 20	# months in school 21	Can read 22	Can write 23	Speaks English 24	25	26	27	28

1910 Census

Local Community _____
Ward _____
Enumerator _____

County _____
[Official census day—15 April 1910]
Date Census Taken _____

State _____
Supervisor's District # _____
Enumeration District # _____

Page No.	Street	House No.	Dwelling No. (1)	Family No. (2)	Name of each person whose place of abode on 15 April 1910 was in this family (3)	Relationship (4)	Sex (5)	Color (6)	Age (7)	Marital status (8)	#Years—Present Marriage (9)	Mother of how many children? (10)	# living children (11)	Birthplace of This Person (12)	Birthplace of Father (13)	Birthplace of Mother (14)	Year of Immigration (15)	Naturalized or alien? (16)	Speaks English? If not, give name of language. (17)	Profession or Occupation & nature of business (18)	(19)	Employer or Wage Earner or Working on Own Account (20)	Out of work 15 April 1910? (21)	# weeks out of work in 1909 (22)	Can read (23)	Can write (24)	School since 1 September 1909 (25)	Owned/rented (26)	Owned free or mortgaged (27)	Farm or house (28)	No. of farm schedule (29)	Civil War Veteran (30)	Blind (31)	Deaf & dumb (32)

1910 Census

Local Community _____
Ward _____
Enumerator _____

County _____
[Official census day—15 April 1910]
Date Census Taken _____

State _____
Supervisor's District # _____
Enumeration District # _____

Page No.	Street	House No.	1 Dwelling No.	2 Family No.	3 Name of each person whose place of abode on 15 April 1910 was in this family	4 Relationship	5 Sex	6 Color	7 Age	8 Marital status	9 # Years—Present Marriage	10 Mother of how many children?	11 # living children	Birthplace of 12 This Person	13 Father	14 Mother	15 Year of Immigration	16 Naturalized or alien?	17 Speaks English? If not, give name of language.	18/19 Profession or Occupation & nature of business	20 Employer or Wage Earner or Working on Own Account	21 Out of work 15 April 1910?	22 # weeks out of work in 1909	23 Can read	24 Can write	25 School since 1 September 1909	26 Owned/rented	27 Owned free or mortgaged	28 Farm or house	29 No. of farm schedule	30 Civil War Veteran	31 Blind	32 Deaf & dumb

1910 Census

Local Community _____

Ward _____

Enumerator _____

County _____

[Official census day—15 April 1910]

Date Census Taken _____

State _____

Supervisor's District # _____

Enumeration District # _____

Page No.	Street	House No.	Dwelling No. 1	Family No. 2	Name of each person whose place of abode on 15 April 1910 was in this family 3	Relationship 4	Sex 5	Color 6	Age 7	Marital status 8	# Years—Present Marriage 9	Mother of how many children? 10	# living children 11	Birthplace of This Person 12	Birthplace of Father 13	Birthplace of Mother 14	Year of Immigration 15	Naturalized or alien? 16	Speaks English? If not, give name of language. 17	Profession or Occupation & nature of business 18	19	Employer or Wage Earner or Working on Own Account 20	Out of work 15 April 1910? 21	# weeks out of work in 1909 22	Can read 23	Can write 24	School since 1 September 1909 25	Owned/rented 26	Owned free or mortgaged 27	Farm or house 28	No. of farm schedule 29	Civil War Veteran 30	Blind 31	Deaf & dumb 32

1910 Census

Local Community ————

Ward ————

Enumerator ————

County ———— State ————

[Official census day—15 April 1910]

Date Census Taken ————

Supervisor's District # ————

Enumeration District # ————

Page No.	Street	House No.	1 Dwelling No.	2 Family No.	3 Name of each person whose place of abode on 15 April 1910 was in this family	4 Relationship	5 Sex	6 Color	7 Age	8 Marital status	9 # Years—Present Marriage	10 Mother of how many children?	11 # living children	Birthplace of 12 This Person	13 Father	14 Mother	15 Year of Immigration	16 Naturalized or alien?	17 Speaks English? If not, give name of language.	18 19 Profession or Occupation & nature of business	20 Employer or Wage Earner or Working on Own Account	21 Out of work 15 April 1910?	22 # weeks out of work in 1909	23 Can read	24 Can write	25 School since 1 September 1909	26 Owned/rented	27 Owned free or mortgaged	28 Farm or house	29 No. of farm schedule	30 Civil War Veteran	31 Blind	32 Deaf & dumb

1910 Census

Local Community ——————

Ward ——————

Enumerator ——————

County ——————

[Official census day—15 April 1910]

Date Census Taken ——————

State ——————

Supervisor's District # ——————

Enumeration District # ——————

		Name of each person whose place of abode on 15 April 1910 was in this family										Birthplace of						Profession or Occupation & nature of business												
Page No.	Street	House No.	Dwelling No.	Family No.		Relationship	Sex	Color	Age	Marital status	# Years—Present Marriage	Mother of how many children?	# living children	This Person	Father	Mother	Year of Immigration	Naturalized or alien?	Speaks English? If not, give name of language.			Employer or Wage Earner or Working on Own Account	Out of work 15 April 1910?	# weeks out of work in 1909	Can read	Can write	School since 1 September 1909	Owned/rented	Owned free or mortgaged	Farm or house	No. of farm schedule	Civil War Veteran	Blind	Deaf & dumb
		1		2	3	4	5	6	7	8	9	10	11	12	13	14	15	16	17	18	19	20	21	22	23	24	25	26	27	28	29	30	31	32

1920 Census

Local Community ——————
Ward ——————
Enumerator ——————

County ——————
[Official census day—1 January 1920]
Date Census Taken ——————

State ——————
Supervisor's District # ——————
Enumeration District # ——————

Page No.	Street 1	House No. 2	Dwelling No. 3	Family No. 4	Name of each person whose place of abode on 1 Jan 1920 was in this family 5	Relationship 6	Own or rent home 7	Owned free or mortgaged 8	Sex 9	Color or race 10	Age 11	Marital status 12	Immigration year 13	Naturalized or alien? 14	Naturalization year 15	School since 1 Sept 1919 16	Can read 17	Can write 18	Birthplace of — This person 19	Mother tongue 20	Father 21	Mother tongue 22	Mother 23	Mother tongue 24	Speaks English? 25	Profession or Occupation & nature of business 26 / 27	Employer, wage earner, or self-employed 28	No. of farm schedule 29

1920 Census

Local Community _____

Ward _____

Enumerator _____

County _____

[Official census day—1 January 1920]

Date Census Taken _____

State _____

Supervisor's District # _____

Enumeration District # _____

Page No.	Street (1)	House No. (2)	Dwelling No. (3)	Family No. (4)	Name of each person whose place of abode on 1 Jan 1920 was in this family (5)	Relationship (6)	Own or rent home (7)	Owned free or mortgaged (8)	Sex (9)	Color or race (10)	Age (11)	Marital status (12)	Immigration year (13)	Naturalized or alien? (14)	Naturalization year (15)	School since 1 Sept 1919 (16)	Can read (17)	Can write (18)	Birthplace of — This person (19)	Mother tongue (20)	Father (21)	Mother tongue (22)	Mother (23)	Mother tongue (24)	Speaks English? (25)	Profession or Occupation & nature of business (26)(27)	Employer, wage earner, or self-employed (28)	No. of farm schedule (29)

1920 Census

Local Community ———————————

Ward ———————————

Enumerator ———————————

County ———————————

[Official census day—1 January 1920]

Date Census Taken ———————————

State ———————————

Supervisor's District # ———————————

Enumeration District # ———————————

Page No.	1 Street	2 House No.	3 Dwelling No.	4 Family No.	5 Name of each person whose place of abode on 1 Jan 1920 was in this family	6 Relationship	7 Own or rent home	8 Owned free or mortgaged	9 Sex	10 Color or race	11 Age	12 Marital status	13 Immigration year	14 Naturalized or alien?	15 Naturalization year	16 School since 1 Sept 1919	17 Can read	18 Can write	Birthplace of						25 Speaks English?	26 27 Profession or Occupation & nature of business	28 Employer, wage earner, or self-employed	29 No. of farm schedule
																			19 This person	20 Mother tongue	21 Father	22 Mother tongue	23 Mother	24 Mother tongue				

1920 Census

Local Community _____ _____ County _____ State

Ward _____ [Official census day—1 January 1920] Supervisor's District # _____

Enumerator _____ Date Census Taken _____ Enumeration District # _____

Page No.	Street	House No.	Dwelling No.	Family No.	Name of each person whose place of abode on 1 Jan 1920 was in this family	Relationship	Own or rent home	Owned free or mortgaged	Sex	Color or race	Age	Marital status	Immigration year	Naturalized or alien?	Naturalization year	School since 1 Sept 1919	Can read	Can write	Birthplace of						Speaks English?	Profession or Occupation & nature of business	Employer, wage earner, or self-employed	No. of farm schedule
																			This person	Mother tongue	Father	Mother tongue	Mother	Mother tongue				
	1	2	3	4	5	6	7	8	9	10	11	12	13	14	15	16	17	18	19	20	21	22	23	24	25	26 27	28	29

1920 Census

Local Community _____

Ward _____

Enumerator _____

County _____

[Official census day—1 January 1920]

Date Census Taken _____

State _____

Supervisor's District # _____

Enumeration District # _____

Page No.	1 Street	2 House No.	3 Dwelling No.	4 Family No.	5 Name of each person whose place of abode on 1 Jan 1920 was in this family	6 Relationship	7 Own or rent home	8 Owned free or mortgaged	9 Sex	10 Color or race	11 Age	12 Marital status	13 Immigration year	14 Naturalized or alien?	15 Naturalization year	16 School since 1 Sept 1919	17 Can read	18 Can write	Birthplace of						25 Speaks English?	26 / 27 Profession or Occupation & nature of business	28 Employer, wage earner, or self-employed	29 No. of farm schedule
																			19 This person	20 Mother tongue	21 Father	22 Mother tongue	23 Mother	24 Mother tongue				

Pre-1930 Period

Interview with _____

Interviewer, date, place _____

Your age in 1930 _____ or circle as appropriate: child   teenager   young adult   adult

Size of your family in the 1920s: _____. Names of persons in the household & relationship to you:

Residence(s) before 1930, with dates, street, town, state _____

When did the family get any of these "modern conveniences"? Telephone _____ Car _____ Electricity _____
Indoor plumbing _____ Running water in the house _____ Vacuum cleaner _____ Electric fans _____
Washing machine _____ Other?

What kind of cooking stove did you or your mother use before 1930? What kind of refrigeration for food?

How was your house heated in the winter? _____

Did your family own its home? _____ Rent? _____ How much was rent? _____
What can you tell me about your house(s) before 1930? Rooms? Size? One, two or more stories? Wood, brick, etc.?

Did your family ever experience a house fire? _____ flood? _____ other natural disaster? _____ Elaborate.

Were you a student before 1930? _____ How far in school did you go? _____
How far from home was your school? _____
Did you have to buy your books or did the school provide them? _____
What can you tell me about your elementary or high school experiences?

What jobs did family members hold in the 1920s or before? (Did any of the women work outside the home?)

Did you work in the 1920s? Doing what?

How did you decide "what you wanted to be when you grew up"?

What did you do for entertainment in the 1920s or before?

When did you or your family get a radio for the first time? _____ a phonograph? _____
Did anyone in the family play a musical instrument? Who? What?

How often did you go to movies? Favorites?

Did the family have pets? Explain.

What part did sports or games play in your life in this period?

During childhood, what is your earliest memory of home and family? How old were you?

What is your earliest memory of events outside the family? How old were you?

During childhood, what were your favorite toys and games? Did you make any of your own toys?

To what extent were family gatherings part of your life before 1930? Explain.

To what extent were religious activities a part in your life before 1930? Explain.

What, if any, rules governed Sunday or the Sabbath in your home before 1930?

Was dancing allowed in your family? _____ Card playing? _____ Dating without a chaperone? _____
Were family members restricted in what they could read for pleasure?
What other rules or customs governed behavior?

How did your family celebrate or observe birthdays? Christmas or other religious holidays? July 4?

What wedding or funeral customs do you remember in your family or community in this period?

Do you remember when you or your family got a camera for the first time? _____

What kind of transportation did you use most? _____

How did you get to school or work? _____

What did the family do at lunch time? Come home or eat elsewhere? What do you remember about school lunches?

Was the main meal at noon or in the evening? What did you call that meal?

If you lived on a farm, what crops did the family raise? What food?

Did any family members serve in the military in World War I? Who? Where?

How did the family celebrate the end of World War I?

Was this a good period in your life? _____ How did your experiences before 1930 affect your life thereafter?

Depression—1930s

Interview with _____

Interviewer, date, place _____

Your age in 1930 _____ or circle as appropriate: child   teenager   young adult   adult

Size of your family in the 30s _____. Names of persons in the household & relationship to you:

Your residence(s) in the 30s, with dates, street, town, state: _____

Did the family own its home? _____ Rent? _____ How much was rent? _____

Did the family have a telephone? _____ electricity? _____ electric appliances? _____ indoor plumbing and running water? _____

What kind of cook stove was used? _____

Which of these were acquired for the first time during the 1930s?

Were you in school any time in the 30s? _____ What level? _____ How did the Depression affect the students in the family?

How did you or they finance education? (jobs, scholarships, parents, etc.?) _____

Did elementary & high school students have to buy their own books or did the school provide them?

Did you or family members have to drop out of school to work? _____ Temporarily? _____ Permanently? _____

Who in the family held jobs during the 30s? Doing what? How many hours/day or days/week did you or they work?

Did you or family members have trouble finding a job? _____ How were you/they able to find work?

Were wages paid in cash, goods, scrip?

Was the family self-supporting? _____ Did you help support your family? Explain.

Was the family a "do-it-yourself" group? If so, explain. Sewing? Carpentry? Making toys? Etc.

How did you or the family "make ends meet"?

Were you or the family able to buy on credit? _____ What items?

Do you remember prices of any items?

What did you do for recreation or entertainment? _____

Did you go to movies? How often? _____ When did you see your first movie with sound? _____ Title?

First movie in color? _____ Title? Favorite movies, stars?

Did your family own & listen to a radio? _____ Favorite programs?

What part did sports or games play in your life in the 1930s?

If you were a child, what were your favorite toys & games?

Did the family have pets? Explain.

What chores were the children and teenagers expected to do?

To what extent were you involved in religious activities in the 1930s? school activities?

Which social, civic, service, labor, or fraternal organizations were you involved in?

Did you or the family own a car? _____ More than one? _____ What make/model car? _____

Do you remember the price of the car or of gasoline? _____ If you had no car, what kind of transportation did you rely on?

Did you or family members travel? _____ By what means? _____
Were trips mostly for business or pleasure? (Comments are welcome.)

What is your earliest or most vivid memory of home and family? How old were you?

What is your earliest memory of events outside the family? How old were you?

In the 1930s, did the family raise, hunt, make, can, preserve any of its own food? If so, what items?

Which food items were most difficult to obtain? _____ easy to obtain? _____

Which commodities (clothes, appliances, tools, toys, etc.) were most difficult to obtain?

Which were easy to obtain?

Did the family have to sacrifice any luxuries or conveniences during the Depression? Explain.

Did you listen to President Roosevelt's Fireside Chats on the radio? _____ What did you think of him as President during the Depression?

Did you or family members work for any of the New Deal agencies (Works Progress Administration, Civilian Conservation Corps, etc.)? What kinds of jobs? Where?

Did you hear Orson Welles's *The War of the Worlds* on radio on 30 October 1939? _____ What did you think? Did you or family members believe it was true? Why or why not?

How have your experiences during the Depression affected your attitudes and life of the present?

World War II and the 1940s

Interview with _____

Interviewer, date, place _____

Your age in 1940 _____ or age group during the war: child   teenager   young adult   adult

Size of your family in the 40s _____. Names of persons in the household & relationship to you:

Residence(s) during the war _____

Residence(s) after the war (1945-1950) with dates, street, town, state: _____

In the 1940s, did you or your family own your home or rent? _____

Which "modern conveniences" did you or your family have before 1940: telephone; radio; electric toaster, mixer, or vacuum cleaner; washing machine; record player; attic or whole-house fan, etc.?

Did you acquire any of these for the first time after the war and before 1950? _____

Did you or your family acquire television or air conditioning before 1950? _____

After the war, what were some of the first major purchases you or your family made?

Were you or your family part of the "rush to the suburbs" after 1945? _____ When? _____ Where?

Were you a student during the 1940s? _____ What level? _____

Did you or family members pursue higher education during the war? _____ Who? Where?

How did the start of the war change your life or plans?

Your job(s) during the war: _____

What jobs did other family members have?

What kind of work schedule did you have? What were your wages?

Who in the family did wartime volunteer work and what kind? Please be specific.

What did you do for entertainment during the war years?

To what extent were you involved in social, civic, service, labor, or fraternal organizations in the 1940s? Which ones?

If you were a child, what were your favorite toys & games?

Did you or your family own a car? _____ More than one? _____ What make/model? _____

What difficulties did you have in keeping it (repairs, parts, tires, gasoline)?

Were you able to travel for pleasure? _____ By car, bus, train? Destination(s)?

What were you doing when you heard about the attack on Pearl Harbor, 7 December 1941? What was your reaction?

Did you hear Roosevelt's "Day of Infamy" speech on 8 December 1941? _____ What was your reaction?

Were you or family members in military service? Who? Which service? Rank(s)?

Were you or family members volunteers or draftees? _____ When did you or they enter service?

Where were you (they) stationed? Or where did you (they) fight? Please comment.

Did your family raise any of its own food during the war? If so, what items?
Did your family can or preserve any of its own food? If so, what items?

What food items were most difficult to obtain? _____ What food items were easiest to get?
What problems did you have in using ration stamps?

What commodities (clothes, toilet tissue, appliances, tires, toys, gasoline, etc.) were most difficult to get?

What items were not available at all?

Did your area experience blackouts? _____ brownouts? _____ Please comment.

Did you rely more on radio, newspapers, movie newsreels, or friends for news?

If you were a child, what is your earliest memory of home & family? How old were you?

What is your earliest memory of events outside the family? How old were you?

To what extent were you aware of the war?

What was your reaction (or your parents') to Roosevelt's decision to seek a fourth term in 1944?

What was your reaction (or your parents') at the time to dropping the two atomic bombs in Japan?

How did you celebrate the end of the war, either VE or VJ Day? If you were in the military, when did you get home?

After the war, did you or family members have difficulty finding work?

After the war, how was your life different from what it had been in 1940?

How have your World War II experiences affected your attitudes or your life?

Decade of the 1950s

Interview with _____

Interviewer, date, place _____

Your age in 1950 _____ or circle as appropriate: child   teenager   young adult   adult

Size of your family in the 1950s _____. Names of persons in the family & relationship to you:

Residence(s) during the 1950s, with dates, street, town, state: _____

Did your family own its home? _____ How much did the home cost? _____

Did your family rent its home? _____ How much was rent? _____

In what ways was your home different in the 1950s from the 1930s or 1940s?

Did you live in a new house? an older house?

Which conveniences did you or your family get for the first time in the 1950s? When?   washing machine _____, clothes dryer _____, dishwasher _____, electric or gas cook stove _____, vacuum cleaner _____, television _____, air conditioning _____, other?

If you were in school in this decade, what level? _____ Where?

What rules & regulations did your school(s) have?

What job(s) did you or family members have in the 1950s?

When did you get your first job? _____ What were your wages/salary? _____

Did you have any job(s) as a teenager? Elaborate.

What did you do for recreation and leisure activity in the 1950s?

To what extent were sports part of your life in this period? As participant or spectator?

What family rules or restrictions governed dating in the 1950s?

Was dancing allowed in your family or community? _____ If so, what dances did you enjoy?

If you were a child in the 1950s, what were your favorite toys and games?

Did you have and ride a bicycle?

If you had a TV, what rules or restrictions, if any, governed its use?

What were your favorite TV programs?

Favorite movies?

Did you listen to radio in the 1950s? _____ Favorite programs?

Did you buy phonograph records of popular music? _____ of other music? _____

Did you have favorite popular music stars? _____ If so, who? _____

Were you an Elvis Presley fan? _____ Did you go to drive-in movies? _____

What fads or fashions did you enjoy in the 1950s?

What organizations (social, civic, service, labor, or fraternal) were you involved in?

To what extent were religious activities part of your life in the 1950s? Explain.

When and why did you take your first airplane trip? (Even if before 1950) _____

If you were a child or teen, did you get an allowance? _____ How much, how often? _____

What chores, if any, were attached to the allowance? _____

What chores were you or children and teens in your home expected to do in the 1950s?

Do you remember prices of anything, including cars, education, appliances, food?

Which, if any, major news events did you watch on TV? (Eisenhower's inaugurations, Queen Elizabeth II's coronation, the McCarthy hearings, etc.)

Were you or family members in the military during the Korean War (1950-1953)? Elaborate: who, when, where, etc.

What was your reaction to the outbreak of the Korean War so soon after WWII?

Looking back, what differences, if any, do you see between life in the 1940s and the 1950s?

What "firsts" occurred in your life in the 1950s?

What significant events in your life occurred in the 1950s?

How would you characterize the 1950s in your life? How did this decade compare to ones before or after?

Decade of the 1960s

Interview with _____

Interviewer, date, place _____

Your age in 1960 _____ or circle as appropriate: child   teenager   young adult   adult

Size of your family in the 1960s _____. Names of persons in the family & relationship to you:

Residence(s) in the 1960s, with dates, street, town, state: _____

Did your family own its home? _____ When was the home purchased, at what price? _____

Did your family rent its home? _____ How much was rent? _____

Describe your main residence of the decade. What were its outstanding characteristics, features, amenities?

If you were a student during the 1960s, what level, where? _____

What level of schooling did you complete?

What school rules governed dress and behavior for students in your family in the 1960s?

To what extent did your schooling prepare you for your career?

How did you decide what career you would pursue?

What job(s) did you or family members have in the 1960s? Do you remember the level of wages?

If you were a teenager during the 1960s, did you hold any job(s)? Elaborate.

What did you enjoy most for recreation and entertainment in the 1960s?

If you were a child in the 1960s, what were your favorite toys, games, pastimes?

To what extent was television part of your life in the 1960s?

What family rules, if any, governed the use of television in your home?

To what extent were movies, popular music, and radio part of your life in the 1960s?

To what extent were sports part of your life, as participant or as spectator?

What *family* rules, if any, governed dating and teen activities in the 1960s? (use of car, curfew, dress code, etc.)

What fads and fashions did you enjoy in the 1960s?

Were there fads, fashions, or aspects of popular culture you avoided in the 1960s?

Were you or family members considered "hippies" or "flower children"? Explain.

As a child or teen, did you get an allowance? _____ How much, how often? _____

Were chores attached to the allowance? _____ What chores were you or children in your home expected to do in the 1960s?

To what extent were religious activities part of your life in the 1960s?

Which social, civic, service, labor, or fraternal organizations did you participate in?

Did you watch on television or listen on radio to any of these news events? What was your reaction?
    (a) First US manned space flight, May, 1961

    (b) Cuban missile crisis, October, 1962

    (c) US military build-up in Vietnam from 1963 forward

    (d) President John F. Kennedy's death and funeral, November 1963

    (e) Assassination of Dr. Martin Luther King, April, 1968

    (f) Apollo 11 landing on the moon, 20 July 1969

    (g) Other?

Were you or any family members involved in anti-war, feminist, or civil rights demonstrations during the 1960s? Who? Where? Elaborate.

Were you or any family member in the military during the Vietnam war? Who? When? Where? Drafted or volunteer?

Comments?

What "firsts" occurred in your life during the 1960s? (first car, first time to vote, first job, first child, etc.)

What significant events occurred in your own life in the 1960s?

How would you characterize the 1960s in the life of the country? in your personal life?

How did this decade compare to those before or after, in your life?

Family Group Sheet of the _____ Family

Full name of husband	Birth date
	Birth place
	Death date
His father	Death place
	Burial place
His mother with maiden name	

Full maiden name of wife	Birth date
	Birth place
	Death date
Her father	Death place
	Burial place
Her mother with maiden name	

Other Spouses	Marriage date, place, etc.
Source #s	Source #s

Children of this marriage	Birth date & place	Death date, place, & burial place	Marriage date, place & spouse
Source #s			
Source #s			
Source #s			
Source #s			
Source #s			
Source #s			

Source #   Sources (Documentation)

Family Group Sheet of the _____ Family, continued

Father _____ Mother _____

Children of this marriage	Birth date & place	Death date, place, & burial place	Marriage date, place & spouse
Source #s			
Source #s			
Source #s			
Source #s			
Source #s			
Source #s			
Source #s			
Source #s			
Source #s			

Notes

Source #   Sources (Documentation)

Family Group Sheet of the _____ Family

Full name of husband	Birth date	
His father	Birth place	
	Death date	
His mother with maiden name	Death place	
	Burial place	

Full maiden name of wife	Birth date	
Her father	Birth place	
	Death date	
Her mother with maiden name	Death place	
	Burial place	

| Other Spouses | Marriage date, place, etc. |
| Source #s | Source #s |

Children of this marriage	Birth date & place	Death date, place, & burial place	Marriage date, place, & spouse
Source #s			
Source #s			
Source #s			
Source #s			
Source #s			
Source #s			

Source #   Sources (Documentation)

Family Group Sheet of the _____ Family, continued

Father _____ Mother _____

Children of this marriage	Birth date & place	Death date, place, & burial place	Marriage date, place & spouse
Source #s			
Source #s			
Source #s			
Source #s			
Source #s			
Source #s			
Source #s			
Source #s			
Source #s			

Notes

Source #   Sources (Documentation)

Family Group Sheet of the _____ Family

Source #   Source #

Full name of husband	Birth date
	Birth place
	Death date
His father	Death place
	Burial place
His mother with maiden name	

Full maiden name of wife	Birth date
	Birth place
	Death date
Her father	Death place
	Burial place
Her mother with maiden name	

Other Spouses	Marriage date, place, etc.
Source #s	Source #s

Children of this marriage	Birth date & place	Death date, place, & burial place	Marriage date, place & spouse
Source #s			
Source #s			
Source #s			
Source #s			
Source #s			
Source #s			

Source #   Sources (Documentation)

Family Group Sheet of the _____ Family, continued

Father _____ Mother _____

Children of this marriage	Birth date & place	Death date, place, & burial place	Marriage date, place & spouse
Source #s			
Source #s			
Source #s			
Source #s			
Source #s			
Source #s			
Source #s			
Source #s			
Source #s			

Notes

Source #	Sources (Documentation)

Family Group Sheet of the _____ Family

Source #   Source #

	Birth date
Full name of husband	Birth place
	Death date
His father	Death place
	Burial place
His mother with maiden name	

	Birth date
Full maiden name of wife	Birth place
	Death date
Her father	Death place
	Burial place
Her mother with maiden name	

Other Spouses	Marriage date, place, etc.
Source #s	Source #s

Children of this marriage	Birth date & place	Death date, place, & burial place	Marriage date, place & spouse
Source #s			
Source #s			
Source #s			
Source #s			
Source #s			
Source #s			

Source #   Sources (Documentation)

Family Group Sheet of the _____ Family, continued

Father _____ Mother _____

Children of this marriage	Birth date & place	Death date, place, & burial place	Marriage date, place & spouse
Source #s			
Source #s			
Source #s			
Source #s			
Source #s			
Source #s			
Source #s			
Source #s			

Notes

Source #   Sources (Documentation)

Family Group Sheet of the _____ Family

	Birth date
Full name of husband	Birth place
	Death date
His father	Death place
	Burial place
His mother with maiden name	

	Birth date
Full maiden name of wife	Birth place
	Death date
Her father	Death place
	Burial place
Her mother with maiden name	

Other Spouses	Marriage date, place, etc.
Source #s	Source #s

Children of this marriage	Birth date & place	Death date, place, & burial place	Marriage date, place & spouse
Source #s			
Source #s			
Source #s			
Source #s			
Source #s			
Source #s			

Source #   Sources (Documentation)

Family Group Sheet of the _____ Family, continued

Father _____ Mother _____

Children of this marriage	Birth date & place	Death date, place, & burial place	Marriage date, place & spouse
Source #s			
Source #s			
Source #s			
Source #s			
Source #s			
Source #s			
Source #s			
Source #s			
Source #s			

Notes

Source #	Sources (Documentation)

Family Group Sheet of the _____ Family

Source #   Source #

Full name of husband	Birth date	
	Birth place	
His father	Death date	
	Death place	
His mother with maiden name	Burial place	

Full maiden name of wife	Birth date	
	Birth place	
Her father	Death date	
	Death place	
Her mother with maiden name	Burial place	

Other Spouses	Marriage date, place, etc.
Source #s	Source #s

Children of this marriage	Birth date & place	Death date, place, & burial place	Marriage date, place & spouse
Source #s			
Source #s			
Source #s			
Source #s			
Source #s			
Source #s			

Source #   Sources (Documentation)

Family Group Sheet of the _____ Family, continued

Father _____ Mother _____

Children of this marriage	Birth date & place	Death date, place, & burial place	Marriage date, place & spouse
Source #s			
Source #s			
Source #s			
Source #s			
Source #s			
Source #s			
Source #s			
Source #s			
Source #s			

Notes

Source #   Sources (Documentation)

Family Group Sheet of the _____ Family

Source #   Source #

Full name of husband	Birth date
	Birth place
	Death date
His father	Death place
	Burial place
His mother with maiden name	

Full maiden name of wife	Birth date
	Birth place
	Death date
Her father	Death place
	Burial place
Her mother with maiden name	

Other Spouses	Marriage date, place, etc.
Source #s	Source #s

Children of this marriage	Birth date & place	Death date, place, & burial place	Marriage date, place & spouse
Source #s			
Source #s			
Source #s			
Source #s			
Source #s			
Source #s			

Source #   Sources (Documentation)

Family Group Sheet of the _____ Family, continued

Father _____ Mother _____

Children of this marriage	Birth date & place	Death date, place, & burial place	Marriage date, place & spouse
Source #s			
Source #s			
Source #s			
Source #s			
Source #s			
Source #s			
Source #s			
Source #s			

Notes

Source #   Sources (Documentation)

Family Group Sheet of the _____ Family

Source #   Source #

Full name of husband	Birth date
His father	Birth place
	Death date
	Death place
His mother with maiden name	Burial place

Full maiden name of wife	Birth date
Her father	Birth place
	Death date
	Death place
Her mother with maiden name	Burial place

| Other Spouses | Marriage date, place, etc. |

Source #s   Source #s

Children of this marriage	Birth date & place	Death date, place, & burial place	Marriage date, place & spouse
Source #s			
Source #s			
Source #s			
Source #s			
Source #s			
Source #s			

Source #   Sources (Documentation)
_____

Family Group Sheet of the _____ Family, continued

Father _____ Mother _____

Children of this marriage	Birth date & place	Death date, place, & burial place	Marriage date, place & spouse
Source #s			
Source #s			
Source #s			
Source #s			
Source #s			
Source #s			
Source #s			
Source #s			
Source #s			

Notes

Source #   Sources (Documentation)

Family Group Sheet of the _____ Family

Source #   Source #

Full name of husband	Birth date	
	Birth place	
His father	Death date	
	Death place	
His mother with maiden name	Burial place	
Full maiden name of wife	Birth date	
	Birth place	
Her father	Death date	
	Death place	
Her mother with maiden name	Burial place	

Other Spouses	Marriage date, place, etc.
Source #s	Source #s

Children of this marriage	Birth date & place	Death date, place, & burial place	Marriage date, place & spouse
Source #s			
Source #s			
Source #s			
Source #s			
Source #s			
Source #s			

Source #   Sources (Documentation)

Family Group Sheet of the _____ Family, continued

Father _____ Mother _____

Children of this marriage	Birth date & place	Death date, place, & burial place	Marriage date, place & spouse
Source #s			
Source #s			
Source #s			
Source #s			
Source #s			
Source #s			
Source #s			
Source #s			

Notes

Source #   Sources (Documentation)
_____

Family Group Sheet of the _____ Family

		Source #
Full name of husband	Birth date	
	Birth place	
His father	Death date	
	Death place	
His mother with maiden name	Burial place	

		Source #
Full maiden name of wife	Birth date	
	Birth place	
Her father	Death date	
	Death place	
Her mother with maiden name	Burial place	

Other Spouses	Marriage date, place, etc.
Source #s	Source #s

Children of this marriage	Birth date & place	Death date, place, & burial place	Marriage date, place & spouse
Source #s			
Source #s			
Source #s			
Source #s			
Source #s			
Source #s			

Source #   Sources (Documentation)

Family Group Sheet of the _____ Family, continued

Father _____ Mother _____

Children of this marriage	Birth date & place	Death date, place, & burial place	Marriage date, place & spouse
Source #s			
Source #s			
Source #s			
Source #s			
Source #s			
Source #s			
Source #s			
Source #s			
Source #s			

Notes

Source #   Sources (Documentation)

Ahnentafel Table for No. 1 _____

Double a person's number to find the father. Double the number and add 1 to find the mother.

Paternal Line	Maternal Line
Parents	
2	3
Grandparents	
4	6
5	7
Great-Grandparents	
8	12
9	13
10	14
11	15
Great-Great-Grandparents	
16	24
17	25
18	26
19	27
20	28
21	29
22	30
23	31
Great-Great-Great-Grandparents	
32	48
33	49
34	50
35	51
36	52
37	53
38	54
39	55
40	56
41	57
42	58
43	59
44	60
45	61
46	62
47	63

Paternal Line	Maternal Line
Great-Great-Great-Great-Grandparents	
64	96
65	97
66	98
67	99
68	100
69	101
70	102
71	103
72	104
73	105
74	106
75	107
76	108
77	109
78	110
79	111
80	112
81	113
82	114
83	115
84	116
85	117
86	118
87	119
88	120
89	121
90	122
91	123
92	124
93	125
94	126
95	127

Ahnentafel Table for No. 1 _____

Double a person's number to find the father. Double the number and add 1 to find the mother.

Paternal Line	Maternal Line
Parents	
2	3
Grandparents	
4	6
5	7
Great-Grandparents	
8	12
9	13
10	14
11	15
Great-Great-Grandparents	
16	24
17	25
18	26
19	27
20	28
21	29
22	30
23	31
Great-Great-Great-Grandparents	
32	48
33	49
34	50
35	51
36	52
37	53
38	54
39	55
40	56
41	57
42	58
43	59
44	60
45	61
46	62
47	63

Paternal Line	Maternal Line
Great-Great-Great-Great-Grandparents	
64	96
65	97
66	98
67	99
68	100
69	101
70	102
71	103
72	104
73	105
74	106
75	107
76	108
77	109
78	110
79	111
80	112
81	113
82	114
83	115
84	116
85	117
86	118
87	119
88	120
89	121
90	122
91	123
92	124
93	125
94	126
95	127

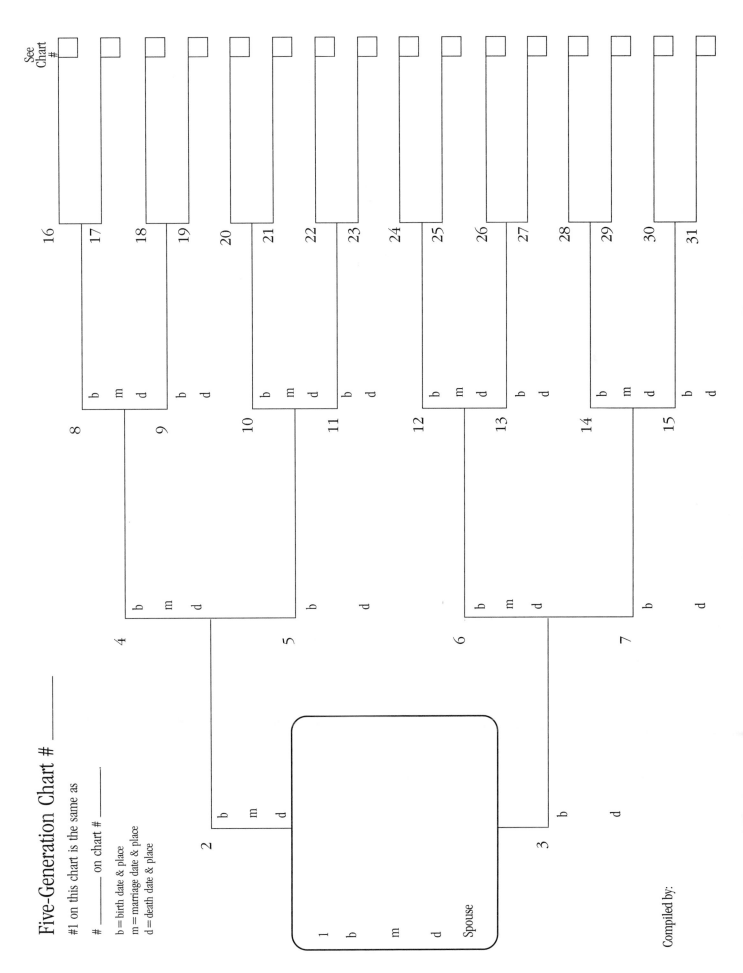

Five-Generation Chart # _____

#1 on this chart is the same as

_____ on chart # _____.

b = birth date & place
m = marriage date & place
d = death date & place

1
b
m
d
Spouse

2
b
m
d

3
b
d

4
b
m
d

5
b
d

6
b
m
d

7
b
d

8
b
m
d

9
b
d

10
b
m
d

11
b
d

12
b
m
d

13
b
d

14
b
m
d

15
b
d

See
Chart
#

16

17

18

19

20

21

22

23

24

25

26

27

28

29

30

31

Compiled by:

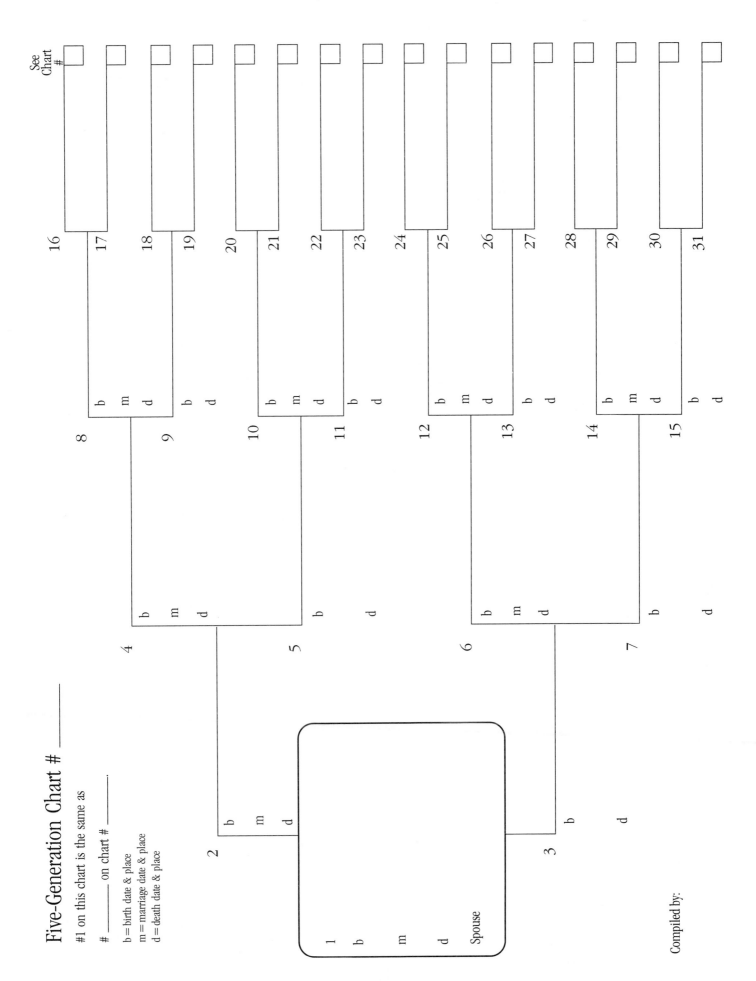

Five-Generation Chart # _____

#1 on this chart is the same as

_____ on chart # _____.

b = birth date & place
m = marriage date & place
d = death date & place

1
b
m
d
Spouse

2
b
m
d

3
b
d

4
b
m
d

5
b
d

6
b
m
d

7
b
d

8
b
m
d

9
b
d

10
b
m
d

11
b
d

12
b
m
d

13
b
d

14
b
m
d

15
b
d

See
Chart
#

16
17
18
19
20
21
22
23
24
25
26
27
28
29
30
31

Compiled by:

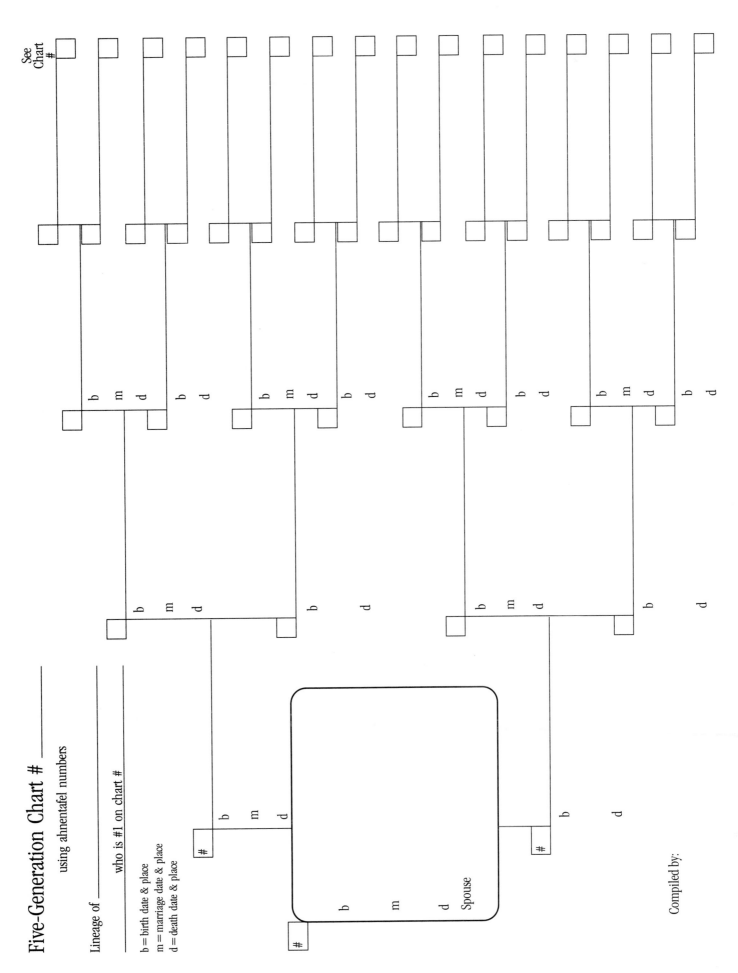

Five-Generation Chart # _____

using ahnentafel numbers

Lineage of _____

who is #1 on chart # _____

b = birth date & place
m = marriage date & place
d = death date & place

See
Chart
#

b
m
d

b
d

b
m
d

b
d

b
m
d

b
d

b
m
d

b
d

b
m
d

b
m
d

b
d

b
m
d

b
d

#

b
m
d

#

b
m
d
Spouse

#

b
d

Compiled by:

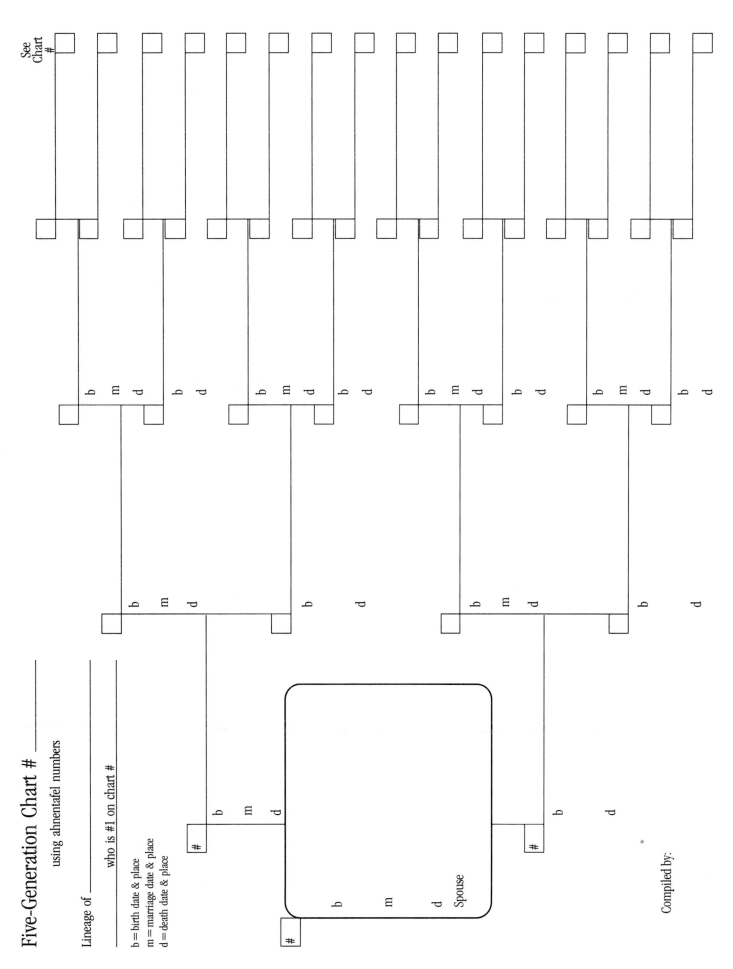

Five-Generation Chart # _____

_____ using ahnentafel numbers

Lineage of _____

_____ who is #1 on chart # _____

b = birth date & place
m = marriage date & place
d = death date & place

See Chart #

Compiled by:

Spouse

Biographical Outline of the Life of _____

With information on education, military service, marriage(s), children, illnesses, religious milestones, migrations, residences, jobs, family events, land purchases, court appearances, death & burial, etc.

Date	Age	Event and Place	Documentation
Birth		Place	

Date	Age	Event and Place	Documentation
Death		Place	
Burial		Place	
Probate		Place	

Biographical Outline of the Life of _____
(Name of person)

With information on education, military service, marriage(s), children, illnesses, religious milestones, migrations, residences, jobs, family events, land purchases, court appearances, death & burial, etc.

Date	Age	Event and Place	Documentation
Birth		Place	

Date	Age	Event and Place	Documentation
Death		Place	
Burial		Place	
Probate		Place	

Biographical Outline of the Life of _____
(Name of person)

With information on education, military service, marriage(s), children, illnesses, religious milestones, migrations, residences, jobs, family events, land purchases, court appearances, death & burial, etc.

Date	Age	Event and Place	Documentation
Birth		Place	

Date	Age	Event and Place	Documentation
Death		Place	
Burial		Place	
Probate		Place	

Biographical Outline of the Life of _____
(Name of person)

With information on education, military service, marriage(s), children, illnesses, religious milestones, migrations, residences, jobs, family events, land purchases, court appearances, death & burial, etc.

Date	Age	Event and Place	Documentation
Birth		Place	

Date	Age	Event and Place	Documentation
Death		Place	
Burial		Place	
Probate		Place	

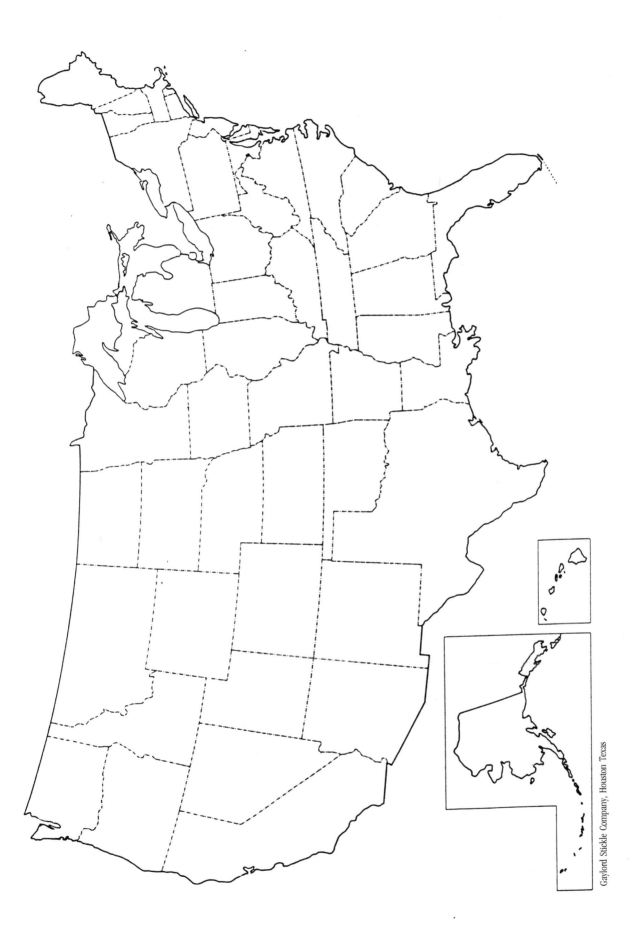

Gaylord Stickle Company, Houston Texas

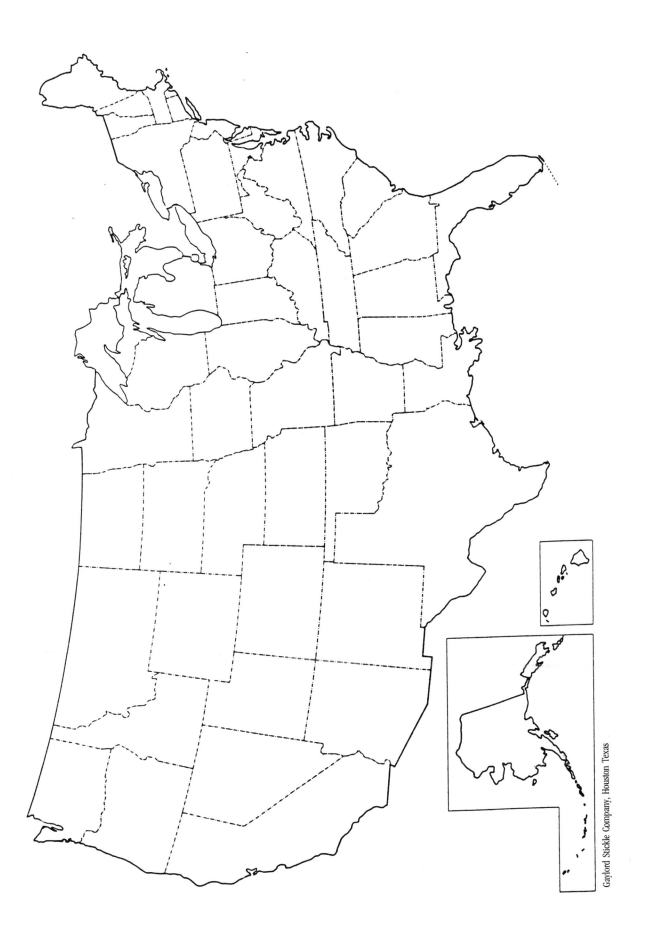

Gaylord Stickle Company, Houston Texas

Family or Surname _____

Timeline 1600-1800

| 1600 | 1625 | 1650 | 1675 | 1700 | 1725 | 1750 | 1775 | 1800 |

- 1607 Jamestown VA founded
- 1620 Pilgrims land at Plymouth MA
- 1630 Massachusetts Bay Colony
- 1634 First settlers to Maryland
- 1642-1649 English Civil War
- 1649 Charles I beheaded. Cromwell & Parliament rule England.
- 1660 Restoration of established 1660 church & monarchy. Charles II crowned.
- 1670 First permanent English settlement in South Carolina
- 1682 Pennsylvania colony begins.
- 1709-1710 First large German immigration (Palatine)
- 1717 Large Scotch-Irish immigration begins, first wave.
- 1733 First settlers to Georgia
- 1754-1763 French & Indian War
- 1763 Treaty of Paris— Britain gets Canada & most land east of Mississippi River
- 1775-1783 American Revolution
- 1788 US Constitution adopted
- 1790 First US federal census

Timeline 1750-1950

Family or Surname

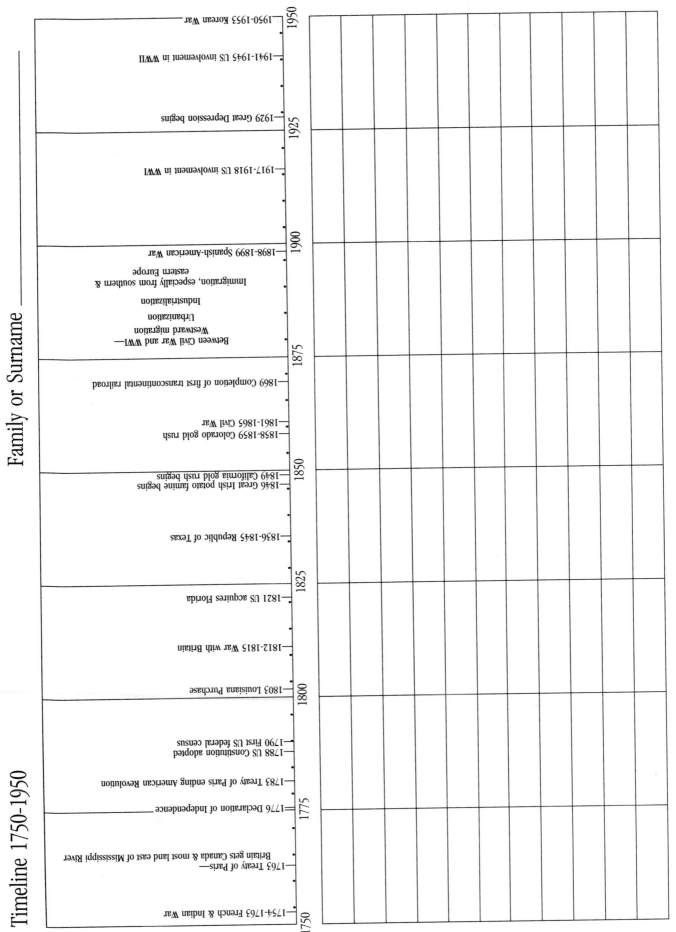

1950 — 1950-1953 Korean War

— 1941-1945 US involvement in WWII

1925 — 1929 Great Depression begins

— 1917-1918 US involvement in WWI

1900 — 1898-1899 Spanish-American War

Immigration, especially from southern & eastern Europe

Industrialization

Urbanization

Westward migration

Between Civil War and WWI—

1875 — 1869 Completion of first transcontinental railroad

— 1861-1865 Civil War

— 1858-1859 Colorado gold rush

1850 — 1849 California gold rush begins

— 1846 Great Irish potato famine begins

— 1836-1845 Republic of Texas

1825 — 1821 US acquires Florida

— 1812-1815 War with Britain

1800 — 1803 Louisiana Purchase

— 1790 First US federal census

— 1788 US Constitution adopted

— 1783 Treaty of Paris ending American Revolution

1775 — 1776 Declaration of Independence

Britain gets Canada & most land east of Mississippi River

—1763 Treaty of Paris

1750 — 1754-1763 French & Indian War